Everyman's Poetry

Everyman, I will go with thee,
and be thy guide

William Blake

Selected and edited by PETER BUTTER

EVERYMAN

J. M. Dent · London

This edition first published by Everyman Paperbacks in 1996
Selection, introduction and other critical apparatus
© J. M. Dent 1996
9 10 8

J.M.Dent
Orion Publishing Group
Orion House
5 Upper St Martin's Lane
London WC2H 9EA

Typeset by Deltatype Ltd, Ellesmere Port, Cheshire
Printed in Great Britain by
Clays Ltd, St Ives plc

British Library Cataloguing-in-Publication
Data is available upon request.

ISBN-13 978-0-4608-7800-5
ISBN-10 0-4608-7800-X

The Orion Publishing Group's policy is to use papers that
are natural, renewable and recyclable products and
made from wood grown in sustainable forests. The logging
and manufacturing processes are expected to conform to
the environmental regulations of the country of origin.

www.orionbooks.co.uk

Contents

Note on the Author and Editor

WILLIAM BLAKE was born in London in 1757, the son of a hosier, and remained a Londoner almost all his life. His parents were Dissenters, and in youth he came under the influence of Swedenborg, later of Boehme and other mystical thinkers. In touch with traditions descending from seventeenth century radical sects he was on the fringe of a circle of radicals of his own day, including Tom Paine and Mary Wollstonecraft. At ten he went to a good drawing school and at fourteen was apprenticed to an engraver. It was as a painter and engraver that he made a precarious living more than by writing.

He married in 1782 and moved to Lambeth (South London) in 1790, where the next seven years were fairly prosperous and very prolific. By the late 1790s his fortunes were declining and he moved to the south coast near a well-intentioned, irritating patron, William Hayley. Returning to London in 1803 he found that his work was too original to be popular. Through years of poverty and obscurity he continued to practise his arts with uncompromising dedication. His life improved after 1818 when he met the young painter John Linnell who commissioned some of his greatest works. Later a group of young artists, including Samuel Palmer, gathered round him, coming to 'the house of the interpreter' – his two-roomed sparsely-furnished flat near the Strand – to hear him talk. By 1827 he was 'feeble and tottering' in body, but 'not in the Real Man the Imagination that liveth for ever'. On his last day of life he 'composed and uttered songs to his Maker', saying to his wife, 'My beloved, they are not mine – no – they are not mine.'

PETER BUTTER, formerly Regius Professor of English at Glasgow University, has written on Romantic, Victorian and modern poetry, especially on Blake, Shelley and Edwin Muir. His editions include Muir's *Complete Poems* (Aberdeen: Association for Scottish Literary Studies, 1991) and Blake's *Selected Poems* (London: Everyman, 1993).

Chronology of Blake's Life

Year	Age	Life
1757		Born 28 November, son of James Blake, hosier, in Broad Street, Soho, London. Parents Dissenters, mother probably connected with Muggletonians, radical 17th century sect
1765–7	*8–10*	Sees angels in a tree, and walking among haymakers
1768–72	*10–14*	Attends Henry Pars's drawing school in the Strand. No other formal schooling
1772–9	*14–21*	Apprenticed to James Basire engraver; makes drawings of monuments in Westminster Abbey
1779	*21*	Student at Royal Academy; exhibits there in 1780. Making living as engraver
1782	*24*	Marries Catherine Boucher (b. 1762), daughter of a market-gardener in Battersea. No children. She helps colour his pictures
1783	*26*	*Poetical Sketches* printed with help of sculptor friend Flaxman and of Rev. A. S. Mathew, at whose house he meets artists and writers

Chronology of his Times

Year	Artistic Context	Historical Events
1759	Birth of Burns	
1760	MacPherson, first 'Ossian' poems	Wedgwood's pottery founded
1765	Percy, *Reliques of Ancient Poetry*	
1769		Arkwright's first spinning mill
1770	Birth of Wordsworth Death of Chatterton (his 'Rowley' poems written 1765–70, published 1777)	
1774–83		Development of Watt's steam engine
1775–83		American Revolution, leading to American independence in 1783
1779–81	Johnson, *Lives of the Poets*	
1780		Gordon Riots in London ('No Popery'); attack on Newgate prison seen by Blake
1783	Crabbe, *The Village*	

Year	Age	Life
1784	26	Death of father. Sets up print shop with fellow Basire apprentice James Parker. Buys a printing press
1784–5	26–7	*Island in the Moon* written, not published
1787	29	Death of favourite brother Robert (b. 1759)
1788	30	First works in illuminated printing – *All Religions Are One* and *There Is No Natural Religion*
1789	31	*Tiriel* written, not published; *Songs of Innocence* and *Thel* etched
1790	32	Moves to Lambeth; severs partnership with Parker
1790–?93	32–5	*Marriage of Heaven and Hell*
1791	33	*The French Revolution* printed, not published
1793	35	*For Children: The Gates of Paradise* (written 1787–93), *Visions of the Daughters of Albion, America, Songs of Experience* advertised for sale
1794	36	*Europe* and *Book of Urizen* *Songs of Innocence and of Experience* brought together
1795	37	*Song of Los, Book of Los* and *Book of Ahania*
1795–7	37–9	Draws copious illustrations to Young's *Night Thoughts*, published incompletely and unsuccessfully in 1797; career as engraver damaged

Year	Artistic Context	Historical Events
1785	Cowper, *The Task*	
1786	Burns, *Poems Chiefly in the Scottish Dialect* Mozart, *Marriage of Figaro*	
1787		Committee for the Abolition of the Slave Trade formed
1788	Birth of Byron	
1789	Bentham, *Introduction to the Principles of Morals and Legislation*	Meeting of Swedenborgian New Jerusalem Church in London; French Revolution, storming of the Bastille
1791	Burke, *Reflections on the Revolution in France* E. Darwin, *Botanic Garden* with engravings by Blake	September massacres in France
1791–2	Paine, *Rights of Man*	
1792	Wollstonecraft, *A Vindication of the Rights of Woman*	Invasion of France by Austria, Prussia defeated
1793	Godwin, *Inquiry Concerning Political Justice*	King Louis executed; Reign of Terror England at war with France
1794		Suspension of Habeas Corpus; Pitt Prime Minister (until 1801)
1794–5		Robespierre executed; Jacobins succeeded by the Directory
1795	Birth of Keats	Napoleon commander in Italy

Year	Age	Life
1797	39	Begins *Vala*, later titled *The Four Zoas*
1799	41	Makes pictures, mainly of Biblical subjects for Thomas Butts, who remains a generous patron until 1810
1800–3	42–5	At Felpham on Sussex coast works on projects for William Hayley, on illustrations to Milton's *Comus*, on *Vala* and probably *Milton*; learns Greek, Latin and Hebrew
1803	45	Fracas with a soldier, leading to trial for sedition; acquitted 1804. Moves back to central London for the rest of his life
1804	46	Title pages of *Milton* (completed *c.* 1810) and *Jerusalem* (completed *c.* 1820) etched; *The Four Zoas* eventually (?1807) abandoned
1805	47	Makes designs for Blair's *The Grave*; the more lucrative engraving given to Schiavonetti. Water colour illustrations to Gray's *Poems* completed
1809	51	Unsuccessful exhibition of his paintings. For next decade suffers poverty and neglect, but continues to do some engraving, and to work on *Jerusalem* and on illustrations to Milton's poems

Year	Artistic Context	Historical Events
1796	Stedman, *Expedition to Surinam* with engravings by Blake	
1798	Malthus, *Essay on the Principle of Population* Wordsworth and Coleridge, *Lyrical Ballads*	
1799		Napoleon First Consul
1802	Scott, *Minstrelsy of the Scottish Border*, followed by own poems (1805–17)	Peace of Amiens
1803		Resumption of war with France General Enclosure Act, simplifying continuing process of enclosing common lands in large farms
1804		Napoleon Emperor; France in control of much of Europe
1805		Battle of Trafalgar
1808	Beethoven, Fifth Symphony	
1809–13		Wellington's successful campaigns against France in Spain and Portugal

Year	Age	Life
1818	60	Meets John Linnell and John Varley for whom he draws 'visionary heads'. *The Gates of Paradise* etched and enlarged; *The Everlasting Gospel* begun
1820	62	Makes woodcuts for an edition of Virgil's *Pastorals*. About this time *The Laocoon, On Homer's Poetry* and *On Virgil* etched
1822–5	64–7	*The Ghost of Abel* etched and, for Linnell, illustrations of the Book of Job
1824–7	66–9	Meets Samuel Palmer and becomes inspirer of group of young artists, the 'Ancients'. Makes illustrations to Bunyan's *Pilgrim's Progress* and, for Linnell, over 100 illustrations to Dante's *Divine Comedy*. Learns Italian
1827	69	Dies 12 August

Year	Artistic Context	Historical Events
1811	Jane Austen, *Sense and Sensibility*; other novels 1813–17	
1812	Byron, *Childe Harold's Pilgrimage*; other poems 1815–24	
1812–13		Napoleon's unsuccessful invasion of Russia
1813	Turner, 'Frosty Morning'	
1814	Scott, *Waverley*; other novels 1815–32	Napoleon's first abdication
1815		Napoleon's escape from Elba; final defeat at Waterloo
1816	Shelley, *Alastor*; other poems 1817–22	
1817	Keats, *Endymion*; other poems 1817–20	
1819		'Peterloo' massacre
1820–21		Revolutionary outbreaks in Spain, Portugal, Piedmont, Greece
1823	Constable, 'Hay Wain' Lamb, 'Essays of Elia'	
1824	Death of Byron at Missolonghi during Greek war of liberation (1821–30)	
1825	Hazlitt, *The Spirit of the Age*	Stockton to Darlington railway line opened

Introduction

Samuel Palmer, who knew Blake well in his last years, wrote that the poet was 'gentle and affectionate, loving to be with little children, and to talk about them. "That is heaven," he said to a friend, leading him to a window and pointing to a group of them at play.' No other poet conveys more beautifully than Blake in his *Songs of Innocence* the sense that heaven lies about us – and not only in our infancy. The poems are mainly spoken by or to children; but there are also protective adults able to share their joy. And Blake retained his powers in old age more than Wordsworth. Palmer says: 'He was energy itself, and shed around him a kindling influence; an atmosphere of life, full of the ideal. To walk with him in the country was to perceive the soul of beauty through the forms of matter.' The *Songs of Innocence* were inspired partly by the young Blake's walks from the centre of the much smaller London of those days into the open country surrounding it, and mainly by his visionary power which enabled him not to escape into a dream world but to see 'the infinite in all things' – in ordinary things.

Songs of Innocence and of Experience may be compared to other volumes of hymns and songs for children popular at the time, which Blake uses, transforms, subtly undermines. With Blake, unlike the usual missionary hymns, it is the black boy who leads the white one to God. The divine image is to be seen and loved in the human form, in 'heathen, turk or jew', and in 'A Cradle Song' the mother sees the divine image in her child rather than, as in Watts's 'Cradle Hymn', contrasting her child to the child Jesus. These poems quietly subvert the orthodox, moralistic poems from which they in part derive; and are far more subtle in rhythm as well as in content. They avoid sentimentality because they contain an awareness of sorrows. 'Innocence dwells with Wisdom, but never with Ignorance', Blake later wrote; and in 1788, at the age of thirty-one, he was by no means ignorant, having seen much poverty and suffering in the central London where he lived and having just written one of the most sombre of his works, *Tiriel*. The light shines more brightly against a dark background. The little boy is lost and weeping (there are more tears in these songs than in *Songs of Experience*) before being found by the father; the little sweep was sold when very young and sleeps in soot; in 'The Ecchoing Green' the sports have an end, the green darkens, and in the illustration an adolescent girl puts up her hand to pluck grapes, suggesting a wish to move on into adult experience. Innocence is shadowed; experience must be entered.

A story retailed by Swinburne shows another side of Blake: 'Seeing once, somewhere about St Giles's, a wife knocked about by some husband or other violent person, in the open street [he] fell with such counter violence of reckless and raging rebukes upon the poor ruffian, that he recoiled and collapsed . . . persuaded . . . that the very devil himself had flown upon him in defence of the woman; such Tartarean overflow of execration and objurgation had issued from the mouth of her champion.'

Blake was a man of extremes, and his *Songs of Experience* are in extreme contrast to the earlier Songs. One of the best is 'London', in which the speaker, wandering through the city, sees nothing but weakness and woe in every face, and hears nothing but the cries of chimney-sweep, soldier (presumably wounded in the wars) and harlot, menacing church, palace, marriage and conventional morality. The picture is unremittingly dark. Are we to say, then, that Blake has grown up to realise what the world is really like, and to repudiate as illusions the visions of his youth? That would be to identify the speaker of 'London' with the poet. No doubt Blake *did* see and hear all that his poem shows and wished to destroy institutions and attitudes which he saw as oppressive, but nearly all his Songs are dramatic – either spoken by children, mothers, nurses, etc., or, if by an 'I', from a specific point of view, designed to show the contrary states of the human soul, not the poet's whole vision. When illustrating 'London', Blake showed that he knew his speaker's vision to be limited. He drew, at the top of the plate, an old man on crutches being led by a small boy, and at the side another boy warming his hands by a leaping flame. Young life, warmth, help are present even in this murky scene. Innocence has not been extinguished.

When gathering the two sets of Songs into one, Blake wrote on the new title page that they show 'the Two Contrary States of the Human Soul'. But there are really more than two. The *Songs of Experience* alone include different states. The state of the nurse in the second 'Nurse's Song' is a wholly negative one, harmful to herself as well as to the children. It is what Blake will later call a Negation, something to be swept away (though the individual temporarily in that state is not to be). But what about 'The Tyger'? Do we not feel the tiger to be wonderful as well as dangerous, and marvel at the daring and skill of the creator and at a universe which contains both tigers and lambs? Surely we do not want a world inhabited only by lambs? The poem consists entirely of questions, and the reader should be content to interrogate a paradoxical world without imposing answers. Nevertheless, we feel in touch with more positive forces than are found in the nurse.

'The Tyger' is about tigers and lambs. With Blake's poetry, we should always start simply, with the literal and the obvious. Yet, remembering that the poem was written during the French Revolution, we may feel it to be connected with the eruption of violent, frightening but possibly cleansing forces at that time. And, reading elsewhere in Blake of 'the tigers of wrath', we may connect it also with forces in ourselves. Certainly, the poem raises cosmic questions. Who is the creator? He is different by far from the effortless, omnipotent creator of Genesis. Is he benevolent? Did he, like the Biblical creator, see that his work was good? *Was* it good? We glimpse in this early poem the several layers of meaning which will become more clearly present in later poems – literal, political, psychological and cosmic.

Having enjoyed the radiance and the dark power of the Songs, many readers are sorry to find Blake developing a complicated and shifting mythology and writing ever longer and more difficult poems. But a great artist never stands still. Having shown, separately, contrary states of being and ways of seeing, Blake needed to explore how they came to be and how they are related; to explore man's fallen state of strife and inner division, and how he might get out of it. These themes are too large for the lyric form. Blake became the greatest, most continuously inventive of English myth-makers. His oddly-named 'characters' at first seem strange and alien, but we soon come to recognise them as aspects of ourselves, of our inner lives, as well as representative of the forces always active behind the events of history.

There is not space here to follow Blake's explorations in full, but we can test the water by looking briefly at one passage which is reminiscent of 'London'. In plate 31 of his longest and probably greatest poem *Jerusalem* another observer, Los the eternal prophet, is sent wandering through London. Now there are no street cries, no blackening church, not much appeal to the senses. Most readers will probably find this passage less immediately appealing than 'London'. But Los's understanding of what he sees is far more penetrating and comprehensive than the earlier speaker's. He has a greater inward understanding of the woes the 'London' speaker only *saw* in the faces. He sees a city in which people are both lonely and crushed into a mass, dehumanized; and he wants to find the criminals who are responsible for this situation. But unlike the earlier speaker who ended on a note of menace, he comes to realise that even if he could find the criminals he 'could not dare to take vengeance', punishing the already punished. Who deserves pity if not the sinner?

In the difference between these two speakers, Blake's own difficult spiritual journey can be traced. Even late in his life he still felt the same passionate anger against oppression that enabled him to rout the ruffian. Yet the central emphasis in his late works is on forgiveness – though not at all an easy, complacent forgiveness. At this time, Blake's external life seemed to be a failure. Coming back to London in 1803 from his 'three years slumber' in Sussex, he found little employment as an engraver; his work lacked fashionable elegance. His 1809 exhibition of his pictures was a complete failure. The prophetic message in his writings was heard by very few, understood probably by none. He was poor. Yet he was able to say to a pretty young girl at a party: 'May God make this world to you, my child, as beautiful as it has been to me.' She thought it strange at the time, she said, that such a poor old man, dressed in such shabby clothes, could imagine the world had ever been so beautiful to him as it must be to her, nursed in all the elegancies and luxury of wealth; but in after years she understood well enough what Blake meant and treasured the few words he had spoken to her.

The passage from *Jerusalem* 31 impresses us less at first than 'London'; but it grows more as one thinks about it. The introductory poem to *Milton*, commonly called 'Jerusalem', combines some of the best features of Blake's early and late writing. We enjoy it immediately, are carried away by its verve and, in the main, understand it. If we are able to place it in the context of Blake's mythology we can see within it more, and more precise meanings. If the mills were simply 'dark', the main point would be adequately conveyed, the mills of industrial England seen to cloud the hills and enslave the people in repetitive labour. That they are also 'Satanic' opens wider perspectives. The mills of Satan are, we can understand from other passages in *Milton*, unimaginative religions, philosophies and scientific theories which, for Blake, lie behind inhumane social and industrial practices. To grow in understanding we have to work to learn Blake's symbolic language; for instance, to discover what he means by Jerusalem. But we do not need to achieve that in order to get enormous pleasure from Blake's poetry.

For many, Blake is more than a great poet. We find his life and work, both humanly flawed, an inspiration; his radical Christianity wiser than orthodoxy. For this selection of his poetry, I have chosen extracts from the prophetic books which I hope can be enjoyed and to a large extent understood on their own. I trust the reader will enjoy them, and not worry if she/he does not fully understand: the learned commentators don't either.

PETER BUTTER

William Blake

from **Poetical Sketches**

To The Evening Star

Thou fair-hair'd angel of the evening,
Now, whilst the sun rests on the mountains, light
Thy bright torch of love; thy radiant crown
Put on, and smile upon our evening bed!
Smile on our loves, and while thou drawest the   5
Blue curtains of the sky, scatter thy silver dew
On every flower that shuts its sweet eyes
In timely sleep. Let thy west wind sleep on
The lake; speak silence with thy glimmering eyes,
And wash the dusk with silver. Soon, full soon,   10
Dost thou withdraw; then the wolf rages wide,
And the lion glares thro' the dun forest:
The fleeces of our flocks are cover'd with
Thy sacred dew: protect them with thine influence.

Song

How sweet I roam'd from field to field
    And tasted all the summer's pride,
Till I the prince of love beheld
    Who in the sunny beams did glide!

He shew'd me lilies for my hair,   5
    And blushing roses for my brow;

He led me through his gardens fair,
   Where all his golden pleasures grow.

With sweet May dews my wings were wet,
   And Phœbus fir'd my vocal rage;   10
He caught me in his silken net,
   And shut me in his golden cage.

He loves to sit and hear me sing,
   Then, laughing, sports and plays with me;
Then stretches out my golden wing,   15
   And mocks my loss of liberty.

Song

My silks and fine array,
   My smiles and languish'd air,
By love are driv'n away;
   And mournful lean Despair
Brings me yew to deck my grave: 5
Such end true lovers have.

His face is fair as heav'n
   When springing buds unfold;
O why to him was't giv'n,
   Whose heart is wintry cold?   10
His breast is love's all worship'd tomb,
Where all love's pilgrims come.

Bring me an axe and spade,
   Bring me a winding sheet;
When I my grave have made   15
   Let winds and tempests beat:
Then down I'll lie, as cold as clay.
True love doth pass away!

Song

Love and harmony combine,
And around our souls intwine,
While thy branches mix with mine,
And our roots together join.

Joys upon our branches sit,   5
Chirping loud and singing sweet;
Like gentle streams beneath our feet
Innocence and virtue meet.

Thou the golden fruit dost bear,
I am clad in flowers fair;   10
Thy sweet boughs perfume the air,
And the turtle buildeth there.

There she sits and feeds her young,
Sweet I hear her mournful song;
And thy lovely leaves among,   15
There is love: I hear his tongue.

There his charming nest doth lay,
There he sleeps the night away;
There he sports along the day,
And doth among our branches play.   20

Song

I love the jocund dance,
    The softly-breathing song,
Where innocent eyes do glance,
    And where lisps the maiden's tongue.

I love the laughing vale,   5
    I love the echoing hill,
Where mirth does never fail,
    And the jolly swain laughs his fill.

I love the pleasant cot,
    I love the innocent bow'r,   10
Where white and brown is our lot,
    Or fruit in the mid-day hour.

I love the oaken seat
    Beneath the oaken tree,
Where all the old villagers meet,   15
    And laugh our sports to see.

I love our neighbours all,
    But, Kitty, I better love thee;
And love them I ever shall;
    But thou art all to me.   20

Song

Memory, hither come,
    And tune your merry notes;
And, while upon the wind
    Your music floats,
I'll pore upon the stream,   5
Where sighing lovers dream,
And fish for fancies as they pass
Within the watery glass.

I'll drink of the clear stream,
    And hear the linnet's song;   10
And there I'll lie and dream
    The day along:
And, when night comes, I'll go

To places fit for woe,
Walking along the darken'd valley   15
With silent Melancholy.

Mad Song

The wild winds weep,
    And the night is a-cold;
Come hither, Sleep,
    And my griefs infold:
But lo! the morning peeps   5
    Over the eastern steeps,
And the rustling birds of dawn
The earth do scorn.

Lo! to the vault
    Of paved heaven,   10
With sorrow fraught
    My notes are driven:
They strike the ear of night,
    Make weep the eyes of day;
They make mad the roaring winds,   15
    And with tempests play.

Like a fiend in a cloud
    With howling woe,
After night I do croud,
    And with night will go;   20
I turn my back to the east
From whence comforts have increas'd;
For light doth seize my brain
With frantic pain.

from **There Is No Natural Religion**

I. Man's perceptions are not bound by organs of perception; he perceives more than sense (tho' ever so acute) can discover.

II. Reason, or the ratio of all we have already known, is not the same that it shall be when we know more.

III. [*This proposition is missing.*]

IV. The bounded is loathed by its possessor. The same dull round, even of a universe, would soon become a mill with complicated wheels.

V. If the many become the same as the few when possess'd, More! More! is the cry of a mistaken soul; less than All cannot satisfy Man.

VI. If any could desire what he is incapable of possessing, despair must be his eternal lot.

VII. The desire of Man being Infinite, the possession is Infinite & himself Infinite.

Conclusion. If it were not for the Poetic or Prophetic Character the Philosophic & Experimental would soon be at the ratio of all things, & stand still, unable to do other than repeat the same dull round over again.

Application. He who sees the Infinite in all things sees God. He who sees the Ratio only sees himself only.

Therefore God becomes as we are, that we may be as he is.

SONGS OF INNOCENCE AND OF EXPERIENCE

Shewing the Two Contrary States of the Human Soul

Songs of Innocence

Introduction

natural imagery → Romantic Movement

interlaced rhyme
ABABAB — nursery rhyme
simple + predictable

Piping down the valleys wild,
Piping songs of pleasant glee,
On a cloud I saw a child,
And he laughing said to me:

childlike / dreaming language

imagination games

'Pipe a song about a Lamb.'
So I piped with merry chear.
'Piper, pipe that song again.'
So I piped, he wept to hear.   5

skipping rhythm - rhyming

'Drop thy pipe, thy happy pipe,
Sing thy songs of happy chear,'
So I sung the same again,
While he wept with joy to hear.   10

repitition of 'happy' enforces positivity

children are easily amused

'Piper, sit thee down and write
In a book that all may read.'
So he vanish'd from my sight.
And I pluck'd a hollow reed,   15

cleansing the world through his writing

And I made a rural pen,
And I stain'd the water clear,

natural - wild/free imagery (Romanticism)

quite corrupt/heavy

oxymoron

And I wrote my happy songs
Every child may joy to hear.   20

[handwritten: writing for everyone to read — Intention of this "Innocence" Section]

The Shepherd

How sweet is the Shepherd's sweet lot!
From the morn to the evening he strays;
He shall follow his sheep all the day
And his tongue shall be filled with praise.

For he hears the lamb's innocent call,   5
And he hears the ewe's tender reply;
He is watchful while they are in peace,
For they know when their Shepherd is nigh.

The Ecchoing Green

[handwritten annotations: A rhythmic / lyrical poem — harmonious]

[handwritten: Iambic Meter / recollective + thoughtful / fluid / 1st person narrative]

The Sun does arise,   *A*   *[masculine]*   *[Rhyming Couplets → stability]*
And make happy the skies;   *A*
The merry bells ring   *B*
To welcome the Spring;   *B*
The sky-lark and thrush,   *½ rhyme*   *[a disruption]*   5
The birds of the bush,
Sing louder around   *— ? feminine rhyme*
To the bells' chearful sound,
While our sports shall be seen
On the Ecchoing Green.   10

Old John with white hair
Does laugh away care,
Sitting under the oak

Is this 'dystopian' → a picture of the future

Among the old folk.
They laugh at our play,   15
And soon they all say:
'Such, such were the joys,
When we all, girls & boys,
In our youth-time were seen
On the Ecchoing Green.'   20

masculine rhyme mostly

positive + cheerful lexis

Nature is restricting community

title is being 'echoed'

Till the little ones weary
No more can be merry.
The sun does descend,
And our sports have an end:
Round the laps of their mothers   25
Many sisters and brothers,
Like birds in their nest,
Are ready for rest;
And sport no more seen
On the darkening Green.   30

½ rhyme
feminine rhyme
parental restriction
more negative language →
coming to an end
→ childhood ending

1. youth
2. old age
3. death
simile

1. youth natural
2. old age
3. moving poet away from youth — associated with freedom

couplet
closure
→ youth

→ idyllic life
- no restrictions
suggests moving into the 'experience' stage
→ the Palace + Church in London

The Lamb

Little Lamb, who made thee?
Dost thou know who made thee?
Gave thee life & bid thee feed
By the stream & o'er the mead;
Gave thee clothing of delight,   5
Softest clothing, wooly, bright;
Gave thee such a tender voice,
Making all the vales rejoice?
   Little Lamb, who made thee?
   Dost thou know who made thee?   10

   Little Lamb, I'll tell thee,
   Little Lamb, I'll tell thee:
   He is called by thy name,

For he calls himself a Lamb.
He is meek & he is mild,   15
He became a little child:
I a child & thou a lamb,
We are called by his name.
    Little Lamb, God bless thee.
    Little Lamb, God bless thee.   20

The Little Black Boy

My mother bore me in the southern wild,
And I am black, but O! my soul is white;
White as an angel is the English child,
But I am black, as if bereav'd of light.

My mother taught me underneath a tree,   5
And sitting down before the heat of day
She took me on her lap and kissed me,
And pointing to the east began to say:

'Look on the rising sun: there God does live,
And gives his light and gives his heat away;   10
And flowers and trees and beasts and men receive
Comfort in morning, joy in the noon day.

'And we are put on earth a little space,
That we may learn to bear the beams of love;
And these black bodies and this sun-burnt face   15
Is but a cloud, and like a shady grove.

'For when our souls have learn'd the heat to bear,
The cloud will vanish; we shall hear his voice,
Saying: "Come out from the grove, my love & care,
And round my golden tent like lambs rejoice." '   20

[handwritten top margin: Nurse's Song / Little Girl x2]

Thus did my mother say, and kissed me;
And thus I say to little English boy:
When I from black and he from white cloud free
And round the tent of God like lambs we joy,

I'll shade him from the heat, till he can bear
To lean in joy upon our father's knee;
And then I'll stand and stroke his silver hair,
And be like him, and he will then love me.

25

[handwritten right margin: Tyger, Lambs / Minor Abstract / Town Research / Alternative / Interpretations / Divine Image]

The Blossom

Merry, Merry Sparrow,
Under leaves so green,
A happy Blossom
Sees you swift as arrow
Seek your cradle narrow
Near my Bosom.

Pretty, Pretty Robin,
Under leaves so green,
A happy Blossom
Hears you sobbing, sobbing,
Pretty, Pretty Robin,
Near my Bosom.

5

10

[handwritten annotations surrounding the poem:]

or an experienced person reflecting

Narrator is an 'Innocent person' without cynicism

no cynicism

Happiness → accept everything in Innocence → short, identical stanzas

superlative

masculine → sexual imagery / phallic

female genitalia

personal — Blake's own heart?

childlike → metaphor

Pretty, Pretty Robin → Sadness

Utopia/Paradise

Natural Imagery

Utopia is being corrupted / infected

Sex is an act of corruption

Innocence has been left behind / sad at the loss

"Innocence"

Comfort + Security

* Research - Blake believed in "Free Love"

The Chimney Sweeper

When my mother died I was very young,
And my father sold me while yet my tongue
Could scarcely cry "'weep! 'weep! 'weep! 'weep!"
So your chimneys I sweep, & in soot I sleep.

There's little Tom Dacre, who cried when his head,
That curl'd like a lamb's back, was shav'd; so I said,
'Hush, Tom, never mind it, for when your head's bare,
You know that the soot cannot spoil your white hair.'

And so he was quiet, & that very night,
As Tom was asleeping he had such a sight:
That thousands of sweepers, Dick, Joe, Ned & Jack,
Were all of them lock'd up in coffins of black;

And by came an Angel who had a bright key,
And he open'd the coffins & set them all free;
Then down a green plain leaping, laughing they run,
And wash in a river and shine in the Sun.

Then naked & white, all their bags left behind,
They rise upon clouds, and sport in the wind;
And the Angel told Tom, if he'd be a good boy,
He'd have God for his father & never want joy.

And so Tom awoke; and we rose in the dark,
And got with our bags & our brushes to work.
Tho' the morning was cold, Tom was happy & warm;
So if all do their duty, they need not fear harm.

The Little Boy Lost

'Father, father, where are you going?
O do not walk so fast.
Speak father, speak to your little boy,
Or else I shall be lost.'

The night was dark, no father was there;   5
The child was wet with dew;
The mire was deep, & the child did weep,
And away the vapour flew.

The Little Boy Found

The little boy lost in the lonely fen,
Led by the wand'ring light,
Began to cry, but God ever nigh
Appear'd like his father in white.

He kissed the child & by the hand led   5
And to his mother brought,
Who in sorrow pale, thro' the lonely dale,
Her little boy weeping sought.

Laughing Song

When the green woods laugh with the voice of joy,
And the dimpling stream runs laughing by,
When the air does laugh with our merry wit,
And the green hill laughs with the noise of it,

When the meadows laugh with lively green
And the grasshopper laughs in the merry scene,
When Mary and Susan and Emily
With their sweet round mouths sing 'Ha, Ha, He!'

When the painted birds laugh in the shade
Where our table with cherries and nuts is spread,   10
Come live & be merry and join with me,
To sing the sweet chorus of 'Ha, Ha, He!'

A Cradle Song

Sweet dreams, form a shade
O'er my lovely infant's head,
Sweet dreams of pleasant streams
By happy silent moony beams.

Sweet sleep, with soft down   5
Weave thy brows an infant crown.
Sweet sleep, Angel mild,
Hover o'er my happy child.

Sweet smiles, in the night
Hover over my delight.   10
Sweet smiles, Mother's smiles,
All the livelong night beguiles.

Sweet moans, dovelike sighs,
Chase not slumber from thy eyes.
Sweet moans, sweeter smiles,   15
All the dovelike moans beguiles.

Sleep, sleep, happy child.
All creation slept and smil'd.

Sleep, sleep, happy sleep,
While o'er thee thy mother weep.   20

Sweet babe, in thy face
Holy image I can trace.
Sweet babe, once like thee
Thy maker lay and wept for me,

Wept for me, for thee, for all,   25
When he was an infant small.
Thou his image ever see,
Heavenly face that smiles on thee,

Smiles on thee, on me, on all,
Who became an infant small.   30
Infant smiles are his own smiles;
Heaven & earth to peace beguiles.

The Divine Image

To Mercy, Pity, Peace and Love
All pray in their distress;
And to these virtues of delight
Return their thankfulness.

For Mercy, Pity, Peace and Love   5
Is God, our father dear,
And Mercy, Pity, Peace and Love
Is Man, his child and care.

For Mercy has a human heart,
Pity, a human face,   10
And Love, the human form divine,
And Peace, the human dress.

Then every man of every clime
That prays in his distress,

Prays to the human form divine: 15
Love, Mercy, Pity, Peace.

And all must love the human form
In heathen, turk or jew.
Where Mercy, Love & Pity dwell
There God is dwelling too.   20

Holy Thursday

'Twas on a Holy Thursday, their innocent faces clean,
The children walking two & two in red & blue & green;
Grey headed beadles walk'd before with wands as white as snow,
Till into the high dome of Paul's they like Thames' waters flow.

O what a multitude they seem'd, these flowers of London town! 5
Seated in companies they sit with radiance all their own.
The hum of multitudes was there, but multitudes of lambs,
Thousands of little boys & girls raising their innocent hands.

Now like a mighty wind they raise to heaven the voice of song,
Or like harmonious thunderings the seats of heaven among.   10
Beneath them sit the aged men, wise guardians of the poor.
Then cherish pity, lest you drive an angel from your door.

Night

The sun descending in the west,
The evening star does shine;
The birds are silent in their nest,
And I must seek for mine.

The moon, like a flower   5
In heaven's high bower,
With silent delight
Sits and smiles on the night.

Farewell, green fields and happy groves,
Where flocks have took delight;   10
Where lambs have nibbled, silent moves
The feet of angels bright;
Unseen they pour blessing,
And joy without ceasing,
On each bud and blossom   15
And each sleeping bosom.

They look in every thoughtless nest,
Where birds are cover'd warm;
They visit caves of every beast,
To keep them all from harm;   20
If they see any weeping
That should have been sleeping,
They pour sleep on their head
And sit down by their bed.

When wolves and tygers howl for prey,   25
They pitying stand and weep,
Seeking to drive their thirst away
And keep them from the sheep;
But if they rush dreadful,
The angels, most heedful,   30
Receive each mild spirit,
New worlds to inherit.

And there the lion's ruddy eyes
Shall flow with tears of gold,
And pitying the tender cries,   35
And walking round the fold,
Saying: 'Wrath by his meekness,
And by his health sickness,

Is driven away
From our immortal day.   40

'And now beside thee, bleating lamb,
I can lie down and sleep,
Or think on him who bore thy name,
Graze after thee and weep.
For, wash'd in life's river,   45
My bright mane for ever
Shall shine like the gold,
As I guard o'er the fold.'

Spring

Sound the Flute!
Now it's mute.
Birds delight
Day and Night;
Nightingale   5
In the dale,
Lark in Sky,
Merrily,
Merrily, Merrily to welcome in the Year.

Little Boy   10
Full of joy,
Little Girl
Sweet and small;
Cock does crow,
So do you;   15
Merry voice,
Infant noise,
Merrily, Merrily to welcome in the Year.

Little Lamb
Here I am;   20

Come and lick
My white neck,
Let me pull
Your soft Wool,
Let me kiss   25
Your soft face;
Merrily, Merrily we welcome in the Year

Nurse's Song

Quatrains   *Iambic Meter – Thoughtful*
                              + Recollective

When the voices of children are heard on the green
And laughing is heard on the hill,
My heart is at rest within my breast   *masculine*
And every thing else is still.   *rhyme*

'Then come home, my children, the sun is gone down   5
And the dews of night arise; —
Come, come, leave off play, and let us away   *— feminine*
Till the morning appears in the skies.'   *rhyme*

'No, no, let us play, for it is yet day
And we cannot go to sleep;   *masculine*   10
Besides, in the sky the little birds fly   *rhyme*
And the hills are all cover'd with sheep.'

'Well, well, go & play till the light fades away
And then go home to bed.'
The little ones leaped & shouted & laugh'd   *feminine*   15
And all the hills ecchoed.   *rhyme*

Infant Joy

[handwritten: Simple + limited choice of words]
[handwritten: repitition]

'I have no name; *[handwritten: come into the world perfect — but the world shapes the person]*
I am but two days old.'
What shall I call thee?
'I happy am,
Joy is my name.'
Sweet joy befall thee!   5
[handwritten: all masculine rhyme]

Pretty joy! *[handwritten: Shows troubles to come]*
Sweet joy but two days old,
Sweet joy I call thee:
Thou dost smile,
I sing the while,   10
Sweet joy befall thee.
[handwritten: repitition — something perfect]
[handwritten: couplet]

A Dream

Once a dream did weave a shade
O'er my Angel-guarded bed,
That an Emmet lost its way
Where on grass methought I lay.

Troubled, wilder'd and forlorn,   5
Dark, benighted, travel-worn,
Over many a tangled spray
All heart-broke I heard her say:

'O my children! do they cry?
Do they hear their father sigh?   10
Now they look abroad to see,
Now return and weep for me.'

Pitying, I drop'd a tear;
But I saw a glow-worm near,

Who replied: 'What wailing wight   15
Calls the watchman of the night?

'I am set to light the ground,
While the beetle goes his round:
Follow now the beetle's hum;
Little wanderer, hie thee home.'   20

On Another's Sorrow

Can I see another's woe,
And not be in sorrow too?
Can I see another's grief,
And not seek for kind relief?

Can I see a falling tear,   5
And not feel my sorrow's share?
Can a father see his child
Weep, nor be with sorrow fill'd?

Can a mother sit and hear
An infant groan, an infant fear?   10
No, no, never can it be,
Never, never can it be!

And can he who smiles on all
Hear the wren with sorrows small,
Hear the small bird's grief & care,   15
Hear the woes that infants bear,

And not sit beside the nest,
Pouring pity in their breast;
And not sit the cradle near,
Weeping tear on infant's tear;   20

And not sit both night & day,
Wiping all our tears away?
O, no, never can it be,
Never, never can it be!

He doth give his joy to all;   25
He becomes an infant small;
He becomes a man of woe;
He doth feel the sorrow too.

Think not thou canst sigh a sigh
And thy maker is not by;   30
Think not thou canst weep a tear
And thy maker is not near.

O, he gives to us his joy
That our grief he may destroy;
Till our grief is fled & gone   35
He doth sit by us and moan.

Songs of Experience

Introduction

[handwritten annotations surround the poem:]

Experienced / clever man → adds sombre tone

well known / respected writer

more control

Hear the voice of the Bard! *}— sense of time passing*
Who Present, Past, & Future sees,
Whose ears have heard
The Holy Word *→ religious reference*
That walk'd among the ancient trees,   5

(Adam's sin)

→ age / experience

Bard is commanding the people to do this

Calling the lapsed Soul, *— the soul of mankind*
And weeping in the evening dew, *→ night-time*
That might controll
The starry pole, *↓ negative message*
And fallen, fallen light renew! *→ from grace*   10

↓ despair

encouraging people to repent their sins

repitition

O Earth, O Earth return!
Arise from out the dewy grass;
Night is worn,
And the morn
Rises from the slumberous mass.   15

} weary / tired connotations

'Turn away no more.
Why wilt thou turn away? *— Rhetorical question*
The starry floor, *↓ doubt / uncertainty*
The wat'ry shore, *— cynicism*
Is giv'n thee till the break of day.'   20

↓ time running out

↓ only a short time - perhaps until the day the soul dies

Earth's Answer

Earth rais'd up her head
From the darkness dread & drear.
Her light fled:
Stony dread!
And her locks cover'd with grey despair.   5

'Prison'd on wat'ry shore
Starry Jealousy does keep my den;
Cold and hoar,
Weeping o'er,
I hear the father of the ancient men.   10

'Selfish father of men!
Cruel, jealous, selfish fear!
Can delight,
Chain'd in night,
The virgins of youth and morning bear?   15

'Does spring hide its joy
When buds and blossoms grow?
Does the sower
Sow by night?
Or the plowman in darkness plow?   20

'Break this heavy chain
That does freeze my bones around.
Selfish! vain!
Eternal bane!
That free Love with bondage bound.'   25

The Clod and the Pebble

'Love seeketh not Itself to please,
Nor for itself hath any care,
But for another gives its ease,
And builds a Heaven in Hell's despair.'

    So sang a little Clod of Clay   5
    Trodden with the cattle's feet;
    But a Pebble of the brook
    Warbled out these metres meet:

'Love seeketh only Self to please,
To bind another to Its delight;   10
Joys in another's loss of ease,
And builds a Hell in Heaven's despite.'

Holy Thursday

Is this a holy thing to see
In a rich and fruitful land,
Babes reduc'd to misery,
Fed with cold and usurous hand?

Is that trembling cry a song?   5
Can it be a song of joy?
And so many children poor?
It is a land of poverty!

And their sun does never shine,
And their fields are bleak & bare,   10
And their ways are fill'd with thorns;
It is eternal winter there.

For where-e'r the sun does shine,
And where-e'r the rain does fall,

Babe can never hunger there,   15
Nor poverty the mind appall.

The Little Girl Lost

In futurity
I prophetic see
That the earth from sleep
(Grave the sentence deep)

Shall arise and seek   5
For her maker meek,
And the desart wild
Become a garden mild.

———————

In the southern clime,
Where the summer's prime   10
Never fades away,
Lovely Lyca lay.

Seven summers old
Lovely Lyca told.
She had wander'd long,   15
Hearing wild birds' song.

'Sweet sleep, come to me
Underneath this tree.
Do father, mother, weep,
Where can Lyca sleep?   20

'Lost in desart wild
Is your little child.
How can Lyca sleep
If her mother weep?

'If her heart does ake,   25
Then let Lyca wake;
If my mother sleep,
Lyca shall not weep.

'Frowning, frowning night,
O'er this desart bright   30
Let thy moon arise,
While I close my eyes.'

Sleeping Lyca lay,
While the beasts of prey,
Come from caverns deep,   35
View'd the maid asleep.

The kingly lion stood
And the virgin view'd;
Then he gambol'd round
O'er the hallow'd ground.   40

Leopards, tygers play
Round her as she lay;
While the lion old
Bow'd his mane of gold,

And her bosom lick,   45
And upon her neck
From his eyes of flame
Ruby tears there came;

While the lioness
Loos'd her slender dress,   50
And naked they convey'd
To caves the sleeping maid.

The Little Girl Found

All the night in woe
Lyca's parents go
Over vallies deep.
While the desarts weep.

Tired and woe-begone,   5
Hoarse with making moan,
Arm in arm seven days
They trac'd the desert ways.

Seven nights they sleep
Among shadows deep,   10
And dream they see their child
Starv'd in desert wild.

Pale thro' pathless ways
The fancied image strays,
Famish'd, weeping, weak,   15
With hollow piteous shriek.

Rising from unrest,
The trembling woman prest
With feet of weary woe;
She could no further go.   20

In his arms he bore
Her, arm'd with sorrow sore,
Till before their way
A couching lion lay.

Turning back was vain;   25
Soon his heavy mane
Bore them to the ground;
Then he stalk'd around,

Smelling to his prey.
But their fears allay   30

When he licks their hands,
And silent by them stands.

They look upon his eyes
Fill'd with deep surprise,
And wondering behold   35
A Spirit arm'd in gold.

On his head a crown,
On his shoulders down
Flow'd his golden hair.
Gone was all their care.   40

'Follow me,' he said;
'Weep not for the maid;
In my palace deep
Lyca lies asleep.'

Then they followed   45
Where the vision led,
And saw their sleeping child
Among tygers wild.

To this day they dwell
In a lonely dell,   50
Nor fear the wolvish howl
Nor the lion's growl.

The Chimney Sweeper

A little black thing among the snow,   A
Crying 'weep! 'weep!' in notes of woe!   A
'Where are thy father & mother, say?'   B
'They are both gone up to the church to pray. B

'Because I was happy upon the heath   A
And smil'd among the winter's snow,   B

They clothed me in the clothes of death,
And taught me to sing the notes of woe.
'And because I am happy & dance & sing,
They think they have done me no injury;
And are gone to praise God & his Priest & King,
Who make up a heaven of our misery.'

Nurse's Song

When the voices of children are heard on the green
And whisp'rings are in the dale,
The days of my youth rise fresh in my mind,
My face turns green and pale.

Then come home my children, the sun is gone down
And the dews of night arise;
Your spring & your day are wasted in play,
And your winter and night in disguise.

The Sick Rose

O Rose, thou art sick.
The invisible worm,
That flies in the night
In the howling storm,

Has found out thy bed
Of crimson joy;
And his dark secret love
Does thy life destroy.

The Fly

Little Fly,
Thy summer's play
My thoughtless hand
Has brush'd away.

Am not I   5
A fly like thee?
Or art not thou
A man like me?

For I dance
And drink & sing,   10
Till some blind hand
Shall brush my wing.

If thought is life
And strength & breath,
And the want   15
Of thought is death,

Then am I
A happy fly,
If I live
Or if I die.   20

The Angel

I Dreamt a Dream! what can it mean?
And that I was a maiden Queen,
Guarded by an Angel mild:
Witless woe was ne'er beguil'd!

And I wept both night and day,   5
And he wip'd my tears away.

And I wept both day and night,
And hid from him my heart's delight.

So he took his wings and fled;
Then the morn blush'd rosy red;   10
I dried my tears, & arm'd my fears
With ten thousand shields and spears.

Soon my Angel came again;
I was arm'd, he came in vain;
For the time of youth was fled   15
And grey hairs were on my head.

The Tyger

Tyger, Tyger, burning bright
In the forests of the night,
What immortal hand or eye
Could frame thy fearful symmetry?

In what distant deeps or skies   5
Burnt the fire of thine eyes?
On what wings dare he aspire?
What the hand dare seize the fire?

And what shoulder, & what art,
Could twist the sinews of thy heart?   10
And when thy heart began to beat,
What dread hand? & what dread feet?

What the hammer? what the chain?
In what furnace was thy brain?
What the anvil? what dread grasp   15
Dare its deadly terrors clasp?

When the stars threw down their spears
And water'd heaven with their tears,
Did he smile his work to see?
Did he who made the Lamb make thee?   20

Tyger, Tyger, burning bright
In the forests of the night,
What immortal hand or eye
Dare frame thy fearful symmetry?

My Pretty Rose Tree

A flower was offer'd to me,
Such a flower as May never bore;
But I said 'I've a Pretty Rose-tree,'
And I passed the sweet flower o'er.

Then I went to my Pretty Rose-tree,   5
To tend her by day and by night
But my Rose turn'd away with jealousy,
And her thorns were my only delight.

Ah! Sun-flower

Ah, Sun-flower! weary of time,
Who countest the steps of the Sun,
Seeking after that sweet golden clime
Where the traveller's journey is done;

Where the Youth pined away with desire,   5
And the pale Virgin shrouded in snow,

Arise from their graves and aspire
Where my Sun-flower wishes to go.

The Lilly

The modest Rose put forth a thorn,
The humble Sheep a threat'ning horn;
While the Lilly white shall in Love delight,
Nor a thorn nor a threat stain her beauty bright.

The Garden of Love

I went to the Garden of Love,
And saw what I never had seen:
A Chapel was built in the midst, — *have to pay to worship God*
Where I used to play on the green.

And the gates of this Chapel were shut,   5
And 'Thou shalt not' writ over the door;
So I turn'd to the Garden of Love
That so many sweet flowers bore,

And I saw it was filled with graves,
And tomb-stones where flowers should be;   10
And Priests in black gowns were walking their rounds,
And binding with briars my joys & desires.

The Little Vagabond

Dear Mother, dear Mother, the Church is cold,
But the Ale-house is healthy & pleasant & warm;
Besides I can tell where I am used well,
Such usage in heaven will never do well.

But if at the Church they would give us some Ale,   5
And a pleasant fire our souls to regale,
We'd sing and we'd pray all the live-long day,
Nor ever once wish from the Church to stray.

Then the Parson might preach & drink & sing,
And we'd be as happy as birds in the spring;   10
And modest dame Lurch, who is always at Church,
Would not have bandy children nor fasting nor birch.

And God, like a father rejoicing to see
His children as pleasant and happy as he,
Would have no more quarrel with the Devil or the Barrel,   15
But kiss him & give him both drink and apparel.

London

[Handwritten annotations surrounding the poem:]
belongs to gentry / organised / structured
nothing is free
bound to — wealth/control
follow instructions
come to 'expect' what's coming next
Iambic — thoughtful / recollective
Regular rhythm
Interlaced Rhyme
masculine effect of footsteps
repetition → notice - signs
(quatrains)
link to innocence
negative (monosyllabic)
emotive
sore - lexis
5 - paced
psychological binding
hasn't provided for people
sense of
sorrow
condemnation
people who serve the public

I wander thro' each charter'd street,
Near where the charter'd Thames does flow,
And mark in every face I meet
Marks of weakness, marks of woe.

In every cry of every Man,
In every Infant's cry of fear,
In every voice, in every ban,
The mind-forg'd manacles I hear:

How the Chimney-sweeper's cry
Every black'ning Church appalls,   10

And the hapless Soldier's sigh *— not being*
Runs in blood down Palace walls; *treated fairly*

But most thro' midnight streets I hear
How the youthful Harlot's curse *Prostitutes are cursing*
Blasts the new born Infant's tear,   15
And blights with plagues the Marriage hearse.

revolution era

Juxtaposition
Prostitute + Newborn

oxymoron   *normally carriages*

The Human Abstract

Pity would be no more
If we did not make somebody Poor;
And Mercy no more could be
If all were as happy as we;

And mutual fear brings peace,   5
Till the selfish loves increase.
Then Cruelty knits a snare
And spreads his baits with care.

He sits down with holy fears
And waters the ground with tears;   10
Then Humility takes its root
Underneath his foot.

Soon spreads the dismal shade
Of Mystery over his head,
And the Catterpiller and Fly   15
Feed on the Mystery;

And it bears the fruit of Deceit,
Ruddy and sweet to eat,
And the Raven his nest has made
In its thickest shade.   20

The Gods of the earth and sea
Sought thro' Nature to find this Tree;
But their search was all in vain:
There grows one in the Human Brain.

Infant Sorrow

asyndetic listing – build up of tone + emotion → negative words   *rhyming couplets*

"very 'retrospective'"

My mother groan'd, my father wept;   *↓ problems ahead in their lives*
Into the dangerous world I leapt,
Helpless, naked, piping loud.   *vulnerability*
Like a fiend hid in a cloud.   *controversial – God? = characteristics/actions*

restrictions
Struggling in my father's hands,   *of someone with a new* 5
Striving against my swadling bands,   *life-experience*
Bound and weary, I thought best   *controlled – conflict of life*
To sulk upon my mother's breast.

– 1st person narrative   masculine rhyme
giving up – despair   monologue   = iambic

A Poison Tree

I was angry with my friend;
I told my wrath, my wrath did end.
I was angry with my foe;
I told it not, my wrath did grow.

And I water'd it in fears,   5
Night & morning with my tears;
And I sunned it with smiles,
And with soft deceitful wiles.

And it grew both day and night,
Till it bore an apple bright;   10
And my foe beheld it shine,
And he knew that it was mine,

And into my garden stole
When the night had veil'd the pole.
In the morning glad I see   15
My foe outstretch'd beneath the tree.

A Little Boy Lost

'Nought loves another as itself,
Nor venerates another so,
Nor is it possible to Thought
A greater than itself to know.

'And Father, how can I love you   5
Or any of my brothers more?
I love you like the little bird
That picks up crumbs around the door.'

The Priest sat by and heard the child;
In trembling zeal he seiz'd his hair;   10
He led him by his little coat;
And all admir'd the Priestly care.

And standing on the altar high,
'Lo, what a fiend is here!' said he,
'One who sets reason up for judge   15
Of our most holy Mystery.'

The weeping child could not be heard,
The weeping parents wept in vain;
They strip'd him to his little shirt,
And bound him in an iron chain;   20

And burn'd him in a holy place,
Where many had been burn'd before.

The weeping parents wept in vain.
Are such things done on Albion's shore?

A Little Girl Lost

Children of the future Age
Reading this indignant page,
Know that in a former time
Love! sweet Love! was thought a crime.

In the Age of Gold,   5
Free from winter's cold,
Youth and maiden bright
To the holy light,
Naked in the sunny beams delight.

Once a youthful pair,   10
Fill'd with softest care,
Met in garden bright,
Where the holy light
Had just remov'd the curtains of the night.

There in rising day,   15
On the grass they play;
Parents were afar,
Strangers came not near,
And the maiden soon forgot her fear.

Tired with kisses sweet,   20
They agree to meet
When the silent sleep
Waves o'er heaven's deep,
And the weary tired wanderers weep.

To her father white   25
Came the maiden bright;
But his loving look,
Like the holy book,
All her tender limbs with terror shook.

'Ona! pale and weak!   30
To thy father speak.
O the trembling fear!
O the dismal care!
That shakes the blossoms of my hoary hair.'

To Tirzah

Whate'er is Born of Mortal Birth
Must be consumed with the Earth
To rise from Generation free:
Then what have I to do with thee?

The Sexes sprung from Shame & Pride,   5
Blow'd in the morn, in evening died;
But Mercy chang'd Death into Sleep;
The Sexes rose to work & weep.

Thou Mother of my Mortal part
With cruelty didst mould my Heart,   10
And with false self-deceiving tears
Didst bind my Nostrils, Eyes & Ears;

Didst close my Tongue in senseless clay,
And me to Mortal Life betray.
The Death of Jesus set me free: 15
Then what have I to do with thee?

The School Boy

I love to rise in a summer morn,
When the birds sing on every tree;
The distant huntsman winds his horn,
And the sky-lark sings with me.
O! What sweet company.   5

But to go to school in a summer morn,
O! it drives all joy away;
Under a cruel eye outworn
The little ones spend the day
In sighing and dismay.   10

Ah! then at times I drooping sit,
And spend many an anxious hour;
Nor in my book can I take delight,
Nor sit in learning's bower,
Worn thro' with the dreary shower.   15

How can the bird that is born for joy
Sit in a cage and sing?
How can a child when fears annoy
But droop his tender wing,
And forget his youthful spring?   20

O! father & mother, if buds are nip'd
And blossoms blown away,
And if the tender plants are strip'd
Of their joy in the springing day
By sorrow and care's dismay,   25

How shall the summer arise in joy,
Or the summer fruits appear?
Or how shall we gather what griefs destroy,
Or bless the mellowing year
When the blasts of winter appear?   30

The Voice of the Ancient Bard

Youth of delight, come hither,
And see the opening morn,
Image of truth new born.
Doubt is fled, & clouds of reason,
Dark disputes & artful teazing.   5
Folly is an endless maze,
Tangled roots perplex her ways:
How many have fallen there!
They stumble all night over bones of the dead,
And feel they know not what but care,   10
And wish to lead others when they should be led.

A Divine Image

Cruelty has a Human Heart,
And Jealousy a Human Face;
Terror the Human Form Divine,
And Secrecy the Human Dress.

The Human Dress is forged Iron,   5
The Human Form a fiery Forge,
The Human Face a Furnace seal'd,
The Human Heart its hungry Gorge.

from **Blake's Notebook**

(c. 1791–3)

'Never pain to tell thy love'

Never pain to tell thy love,
Love that never told can be;
For the gentle wind does move
Silently, invisibly.

I told my love, I told my love,   5
I told her all my heart;
Trembling, cold, in ghastly fears –
Ah, she doth depart.

Soon as she was gone from me
A traveller came by   10
Silently, invisibly –
O, was no deny.

'I saw a chapel all of gold'

I saw a chapel all of gold
That none did dare to enter in;
And many weeping stood without,
Weeping, mourning, worshipping.

I saw a serpent rise between   5
The white pillars of the door,
And he forc'd & forc'd & forc'd –
Down the golden hinges tore,

And along the pavement sweet,
Set with pearls & rubies bright,   10
All his slimy length he drew,
Till upon the altar white

Vomiting his poison out
On the bread & on the wine.
So I turn'd into a sty   15
And laid me down among the swine.

'I asked a thief to steal me a peach'

I asked a thief to steal me a peach;
He turned up his eyes.
I ask'd a lithe lady to lie her down;
Holy & meek she cries.

As soon as I went   5
An angel came;
He wink'd at the thief
And smil'd at the dame,

And without one word said
Had a peach from the tree,   10
And still as a maid
Enjoy'd the lady.

A Cradle Song

Sleep, Sleep, beauty bright,
Dreaming o'er the joys of night.
Sleep, Sleep; in thy sleep
Little sorrows sit & weep.

Sweet Babe, in thy face   5
Soft desires I can trace,
Secret joys & secret smiles,
Little pretty infant wiles.

As thy softest limbs I feel,
Smiles as of the morning steal   10
O'er thy cheek, & o'er thy breast
Where thy little heart does rest.

O, the cunning wiles that creep
In thy little heart asleep!
When thy little heart does wake,   15
Then the dreadful lightnings break

From thy cheek & from thy eye,
O'er the youthful harvest nigh.
Infant wiles & infant smiles
Heaven & Earth of peace beguiles.   20

'Silent, Silent Night'

Silent, Silent Night,
Quench the holy light
Of thy torches bright;

For, possess'd of Day,
Thousand spirits stray   5
That sweet joys betray.

Why should joys be sweet
Used with deceit,
Nor with sorrows meet?

> But an honest joy   10
> Does itself destroy
> For a harlot coy.

To Nobodaddy

> Why art thou silent & invisible,
> Father of Jealousy?
> Why dost thou hide thyself in clouds
> From every searching Eye?
>
> Why darkness & obscurity   5
> In all thy words & laws,
> That none dare eat the fruit but from
> The wily serpent's jaws?
> Or is it because Secresy
> Gains females' loud applause?   10

'Love to faults is always blind'

> Love to faults is always blind,
> Always is to joy inclin'd,
> Lawless, wing'd & unconfin'd,
> And breaks all chains from every mind.
>
> Deceit to secresy confin'd,   5
> Lawful, cautious & refin'd,
> To every thing but interest blind,
> And forges fetters for the mind.

Eternity

He who binds to himself a joy
Does the winged life destroy;
But he who kisses the joy as it flies
Lives in eternity's sun rise.

Riches

The countless gold of a merry heart,
The rubies & pearls of a loving eye,
The indolent never can bring to the mart,
Nor the secret hoard up in his treasury.

'The look of love alarms'

The look of love alarms
Because 'tis fill'd with fire;
But the look of soft deceit
Shall win the lover's hire.

The Book of Thel

1

PLATE 1
The daughters of Mne Seraphim led round their sunny flocks,
All but the youngest. She in paleness sought the secret air,
To fade away like morning beauty from her mortal day.
Down by the river of Adona her soft voice is heard,
And thus her gentle lamentation falls like morning dew: 5

'O life of this our spring! why fades the lotus of the water?
Why fade these children of the spring, born but to smile & fall?
Ah! Thel is like a wat'ry bow, and like a parting cloud,
Like a reflection in a glass, like shadows in the water,
Like dreams of infants, like a smile upon an infant's face,   10
Like the dove's voice, like transient day, like music in the air.
Ah! gentle may I lay me down and gentle rest my head,
And gentle sleep the sleep of death, and gentle hear the voice
Of him that walketh in the garden in the evening time.'

The Lilly of the Valley, breathing in the humble grass,   15
Answer'd the lovely maid, and said: 'I am a wat'ry weed,
And I am very small, and love to dwell in lowly vales;
So weak the gilded butterfly scarce perches on my head;
Yet I am visited from heaven, and he that smiles on all
Walks in the valley, and each morn over me spreads his hand,   20
Saying: "Rejoice, thou humble grass, thou new-born lilly
     flower,
Thou gentle maid of silent valleys and of modest brooks;
For thou shalt be clothed in light, and fed with morning
     manna,
Till summer's heat melts thee beside the fountains and the
     springs
To flourish in eternal vales." Then why should Thel com-
     plain?   25

PLATE 2
Why should the mistress of the vales of Har utter a sigh?'

She ceas'd & smil'd in tears, then sat down in her silver shrine.

Thel answer'd: 'O thou little virgin of the peaceful valley,
Giving to those that cannot crave, the voiceless, the o'erfired;
Thy breath doth nourish the innocent lamb, he smells thy
    milky garments,   5
He crops thy flowers while thou sittest smiling in his face,
Wiping his mild and meekin mouth from all contagious
    taints.
Thy wine doth purify the golden honey; thy perfume,
Which thou dost scatter on every little blade of grass that
    springs,
Revives the milked cow, & tames the fire-breathing steed.   10
But Thel is like a faint cloud kindled at the rising sun:
I vanish from my pearly throne, and who shall find my place?'

'Queen of the vales,' the Lilly answer'd, 'ask the tender cloud,
And it shall tell thee why it glitters in the morning sky,
And why it scatters its bright beauty thro' the humid air.   15
Descend, O little cloud, & hover before the eyes of Thel.'

The Cloud descended, and the Lilly bow'd her modest head,
And went to mind her numerous charge among the verdant
    grass.

2

PLATE 3
'O little Cloud,' the virgin said, 'I charge thee tell to me
Why thou complainest not when in one hour thou fade away;
Then we shall seek thee, but not find. Ah! Thel is like to thee:
I pass away; yet I complain, and no one hears my voice.'

The Cloud then shew'd his golden head, & his bright form
    emerg'd,   5
Hovering and glittering on the air before the face of Thel:

'O virgin, know'st thou not? Our steeds drink of the golden
    springs
Where Luvah doth renew his horses. Look'st thou on my
    youth,

And fearest thou, because I vanish and am seen no more,
Nothing remains? O maid I tell thee, when I pass away   10
It is to tenfold life, to love, to peace, and raptures holy.
Unseen descending, weigh my light wings upon balmy
    flowers,
And court the fair eyed dew to take me to her shining tent.
The weeping virgin trembling kneels before the risen sun,
Till we arise link'd in a golden band and never part,   15
But walk united, bearing food to all our tender flowers.'

'Dost thou, O little Cloud? I fear that I am not like thee;
For I walk thro' the vales of Har, and smell the sweetest
    flowers,
But I feed not the little flowers. I hear the warbling birds,
But I feed not the warbling birds; they fly and seek their food. 20
But Thel delights in these no more, because I fade away;
And all shall say, "Without a use this shining woman liv'd,
Or did she only live to be at death the food of worms?" '

The Cloud reclin'd upon his airy throne and answer'd thus:

'Then if thou art the food of worms, O virgin of the skies,   25
How great thy use, how great thy blessing! Every thing that
    lives
Lives not alone, nor for itself. Fear not, and I will call
The weak worm from its lowly bed, and thou shalt hear its
    voice.
Come forth, worm of the silent valley, to thy pensive queen.'

The helpless worm arose, and sat upon the Lilly's leaf,   30
And the bright Cloud sail'd on, to find his partner in the vale.

3

PLATE 4
Then Thel astonish'd view'd the Worm upon its dewy bed:
'Art thou a Worm? image of weakness, art thou but a Worm?
I see thee like an infant wrapped in the Lilly's leaf.
Ah, weep not, little voice, thou canst not speak, but thou
    canst weep.
Is this a Worm? I see thee lay helpless & naked, weeping,   5

And none to answer, none to cherish thee with mother's
    smiles.'

The Clod of Clay heard the Worm's voice, & rais'd her pitying
    head;
She bow'd over the weeping infant, and her life exhal'd
In milky fondness; then on Thel she fix'd her humble eyes.

'O beauty of the vales of Har, we live not for ourselves.   10
Thou seest me the meanest thing, and so I am indeed;
My bosom of itself is cold, and of itself is dark,

PLATE 5
But he that loves the lowly pours his oil upon my head,
And kisses me, and binds his nuptial bands around my breast,
And says: "Thou mother of my children, I have loved thee,
And I have given thee a crown that none can take away."
But how this is, sweet maid, I know not, and I cannot know;   5
I ponder, and I cannot ponder; yet I live and love.'

The daughter of beauty wip'd her pitying tears with her white
    veil,
And said: 'Alas! I knew not this, and therefore did I weep.
That God would love a Worm I knew, and punish the evil foot
That wilful bruis'd its helpless form; but that he cherish'd it   10
With milk and oil I never knew, and therefore did I weep;
And I complain'd in the mild air, because I fade away,
And lay me down in thy cold bed, and leave my shining lot.'

'Queen of the vales,' the matron Clay answer'd, 'I heard thy
    sighs,
And all thy moans flew o'er my roof, but I have call'd them
    down.   15
Wilt thou, O Queen, enter my house? 'Tis given thee to enter
And to return; fear nothing; enter with thy virgin feet.'

4

PLATE 6
The eternal gates' terrific porter lifted the northern bar.
Thel enter'd in & saw the secrets of the land unknown.

She saw the couches of the dead, & where the fibrous roots
Of every heart on earth infixes deep its restless twists:
A land of sorrows & of tears where never smile was seen.   5

She wander'd in the land of clouds thro' valleys dark, list'ning
Dolours and lamentations; waiting oft beside a dewy grave
She stood in silence, list'ning to the voices of the ground,
Till to her own grave plot she came, & there she sat down,
And heard this voice of sorrow breathed from the hollow pit: 10

'Why cannot the Ear be closed to its own destruction?
Or the glist'ning Eye to the poison of a smile?
Why are Eyelids stor'd with arrows ready drawn,
Where a thousand fighting men in ambush lie?
Or an Eye of gifts & graces, show'ring fruits & coined gold?   15
Why a Tongue impress'd with honey from every wind?
Why an Ear a whirlpool fierce to draw creations in?
Why a Nostril wide inhaling terror, trembling & affright?
Why a tender curb upon the youthful burning boy?
Why a little curtain of flesh on the bed of our desire?'   20

The Virgin started from her seat, & with a shriek
Fled back unhinder'd till she came into the vales of Har.

THEL'S MOTTO

Does the Eagle know what is in the pit,
Or wilt thou go ask the Mole?
Can Wisdom be put in a silver rod,
Or Love in a golden bowl?

from **The Marriage of Heaven and Hell**

(handwritten annotations: -A03 - Blake is prophecising in this "poem" - about romantic + revolutionary beliefs + personal)

(handwritten: 24 Plates)

(handwritten: written in Prose)

PLATE 3

As a new heaven is begun, and it is now thirty-three years since its *(handwritten: mysticism ↓ Blake believed)* advent, the Eternal Hell revives. And lo! Swedenborg is the Angel sitting at the tomb; his writings are the linen clothes folded up. Now is the dominion of Edom, & the return of Adam into Paradise; see Isaiah xxxiv & xxxv Chap.

Without Contraries is no progression. Attraction and Repulsion, Reason and Energy, Love and Hate, are necessary to Human existence.

From these contraries spring what the religious call Good & Evil. *(handwritten: Good + Evil)* Good is the passive that obeys Reason. Evil is the active springing from Energy. *(handwritten: revolutionary / revolution - religion has prescribed)*

Good is Heaven. Evil is Hell. *(handwritten: re-wrote the Cosmos)*

(handwritten: too simple - incorrect)

THE VOICE OF THE DEVIL

(handwritten: Blake doesn't conform to a religion with "rules")

PLATE 4

All Bibles or sacred codes have been the causes of the following Errors:

1. That Man has two real existing principles, Viz: a Body & a Soul.

2. That Energy, call'd Evil, is alone from the Body, & that Reason, call'd Good, is alone from the Soul.

3. That God will torment Man in Eternity for following his Energies.

(handwritten: not Blake → persona / voice of devil)

But the following Contraries to these are True:

1. Man has no Body distinct from his Soul; for that call'd Body is a portion of Soul discern'd by the five Senses, the chief inlets of Soul in this age.

2. Energy is the only life and is from the Body, and Reason is the bound or outward circumference of Energy.

3. Energy is Eternal Delight. *(handwritten: - prose also has rhythm and rhyme)*

PLATES 5–6

Those who restrain desire do so because theirs is weak enough to be restrained; and the restrainer or reason usurps its place & governs the unwilling.

And being restrain'd it by degrees becomes passive, till it is only the shadow of desire.

The history of this is written in Paradise Lost, & the Governor or Reason is call'd Messiah.

And the original Archangel, or possessor of the command of the heavenly host, is call'd the Devil or Satan, and his children are call'd Sin & Death.

But in the Book of Job Milton's Messiah is call'd Satan.

For this history has been adopted by both parties.

It indeed appear'd to Reason as if Desire was cast out; but the Devil's account is that the Messiah fell, & formed a heaven of what he stole from the Abyss.

This is shewn in the Gospel, where he prays to the Father to send the comforter, or Desire, that Reason may have Ideas to build on, the Jehovah of the Bible being no other than he who dwells in flaming fire. Know that after Christ's death, he became Jehovah.

But in Milton, the Father is Destiny, the Son a Ratio of the five senses, & the Holy-ghost Vacuum!

Note. The reason Milton wrote in fetters when he wrote of Angels & God, and at liberty when of Devils & Hell, is because he was a true Poet and of the Devil's party without knowing it.

A MEMORABLE FANCY

PLATES 6–7
As I was walking among the fires of hell, delighted with the enjoyments of Genius, which to Angels look like torment and insanity, I collected some of their Proverbs, thinking that as the sayings used in a nation mark its character, so the Proverbs of Hell shew the nature of Infernal wisdom better than any description of buildings or garments.

When I came home, on the abyss of the five senses, where a flat sided steep frowns over the present world, I saw a mighty Devil folded in black clouds hovering on the sides of the rock. With corroding fires he wrote the following sentence now perceived by the minds of men, & read by them on earth:

How do you know but ev'ry Bird that cuts the airy way

Is an immense world of delight, clos'd by your senses five?

PROVERBS OF HELL
PLATE 7

In seed time learn, in harvest teach, in winter enjoy.
Drive your cart and your plow over the bones of the dead.
The road of excess leads to the palace of wisdom.
Prudence is a rich ugly old maid courted by Incapacity.
He who desires but acts not breeds pestilence.   5
The cut worm forgives the plow.
Dip him in the river who loves water.
A fool sees not the same tree that a wise man sees.
He whose face gives no light shall never become a star.
Eternity is in love with the productions of time.   10
The busy bee has no time for sorrow.
The hours of folly are measur'd by the clock, but of wisdom no
    clock can measure.
All wholesome food is caught without a net or a trap.
Bring out number, weight & measure in a year of dearth.
No bird soars too high if he soars with his own wings.   15
A dead body revenges not injuries.
The most sublime act is to set another before you.
If the fool would persist in his folly he would become wise.
Folly is the cloke of knavery.
Shame is Pride's cloke.   20

PLATE 8

[handwritten: 7 deadly sins]

Prisons are built with stones of Law, Brothels with bricks of
    Religion. [handwritten: - iambic pentameter]
The pride of the peacock is the glory of God. [handwritten: natural + animalistic imagery]
The lust of the goat is the bounty of God.
The wrath of the lion is the wisdom of God.
The nakedness of woman is the work of God. [handwritten: sadness should be laughed. laughed instead]
Excess of sorrow laughs. Excess of joy weeps.
The roaring of lions, the howling of wolves, the raging of the
    stormy sea, and the destructive sword are portions of
    eternity too great for the eye of man.
The fox condemns the trap, not himself.
Joys impregnate. Sorrows bring forth.

[handwritten: monosyllabic quality]

Let man wear the fell of the lion, woman the fleece of the
    sheep.   10
The bird a nest, the spider a web, man friendship.
The selfish smiling fool & the sullen frowning fool shall be
    both thought wise, that they may be a rod.
What is now proved was once only imagin'd.
The rat, the mouse, the fox, the rabbet watch the roots; the
    lion, the tyger, the horse, the elephant watch the fruits.
The cistern contains; the fountain overflows.   15
One thought fills immensity.
Always be ready to speak your mind, and a base man will
    avoid you.
Every thing possible to be believ'd is an image of truth.
The eagle never lost so much time as when he submitted to
    learn of the crow.

PLATE 9
The fox provides for himself, but God provides for the lion.
Think in the morning. Act in the noon. Eat in the evening.
    Sleep in the night.
He who has suffer'd you to impose on him knows you.
As the plow follows words, so God rewards prayers.
The tygers of wrath are wiser than the horses of instruction.   5
Expect poison from the standing water.
You never know what is enough unless you know what is
    more than enough.
Listen to the fool's reproach! it is a kingly title!
The eyes of fire, the nostrils of air, the mouth of water, the
    beard of earth.
The weak in courage is strong in cunning.   10
The apple tree never asks the beech how he shall grow, nor
    the lion the horse how he shall take his prey.
The thankful receiver bears a plentiful harvest.
If others had not been foolish, we should be so.
The soul of sweet delight can never be defil'd.
When thou seest an Eagle, thou seest a portion of Genius; lift
    up thy head!   15
As the catterpiller chooses the fairest leaves to lay her eggs on,
    so the priest lays his curse on the fairest joys.

To create a little flower is the labour of ages.
Damn braces. Bless relaxes.
The best wine is the oldest, the best water the newest.
Prayers plow not! Praises reap not!   20
Joys laugh not! Sorrows weep not!

PLATE 10
The head Sublime, the heart Pathos, the genitals Beauty, the
    hands & feet Proportion.
As the air to a bird or the sea to a fish, so is contempt to the
    contemptible.
The crow wish'd every thing was black, the owl that every
    thing was white.
Exuberance is Beauty.
If the lion was advised by the fox, he would be cunning.   5
Improvement makes strait roads, but the crooked roads
    without Improvement are roads of Genius.
Sooner murder an infant in its cradle than nurse unacted
    desires.
Where man is not, nature is barren.
Truth can never be told so as to be understood and not be
    believ'd.
Enough! or Too much.   10

PLATE 11
The ancient Poets animated all sensible objects with Gods or
Geniuses, calling them by the names and adorning them with
the properties of woods, rivers, mountains, lakes, cities,
nations, and whatever their enlarged & numerous senses
could perceive.
    And particularly they studied the genius of each city &
country, placing it under its mental deity.
    Till a system was formed, which some took advantage of &
enslav'd the vulgar by attempting to realize or abstract the
mental deities from their objects; thus began Priesthood,
    Choosing forms of worship from poetic tales.
    And at length they pronounc'd that the Gods had order'd
such things.
    Thus men forgot that All deities reside in the human breast.

*

PLATE 14

The ancient tradition that the world will be consumed in fire at the end of six thousand years is true, as I have heard from Hell.

For the cherub with his flaming sword is hereby commanded to leave his guard at tree of life; and when he does, the whole creation will be consumed and appear infinite and holy, whereas it now appears finite & corrupt.

This will come to pass by an improvement of sensual enjoyment.

But first the notion that man has a body distinct from his soul is to be expunged. This I shall do, by printing in the infernal method, by corrosives, which in Hell are salutary and medicinal, melting apparent surfaces away, and displaying the infinite which was hid.

If the doors of perception were cleansed, every thing would appear to man as it is, infinite.

For man has closed himself up, till he sees all things thro' narrow chinks of his cavern.

from **Visions of the Daughters of Albion**

PLATE 5
But when the morn arose, her lamentations renew'd.
The Daughters of Albion hear her woes, & eccho back her
   sighs.

'O Urizen! Creator of men! mistaken Demon of heaven,
Thy joys are tears! thy labour vain to form men to thine
   image.
How can one joy absorb another? are not different joys   5
Holy, eternal, infinite? and each joy is a Love.

'Does not the great mouth laugh at a gift? & the narrow
   eyelids mock
At the labour that is above payment? and wilt thou take the
   ape
For thy counsellor? or the dog for a schoolmaster to thy
   children?
Does he who contemns poverty, and he who turns with
   abhorrence   10
From usury, feel the same passion, or are they moved alike?
How can the giver of gifts experience the delights of the
   merchant?
How the industrious citizen the pains of the husbandman?
How different far the fat fed hireling with hollow drum,
Who buys whole corn fields into wastes, and sings upon the
   heath: 15
How different their eye and ear! how different the world to
   them!
With what sense does the parson claim the labour of the
   farmer?
What are his nets & gins & traps, & how does he surround him
With cold floods of abstraction, and with forests of solitude,
To build him castles and high spires, where kings & priests
   may dwell,   20

Till she who burns with youth and knows no fixed lot, is
    bound
In spells of law to one she loaths? and must she drag the chain
Of life in weary lust? must chilling murderous thoughts
    obscure
The clear heaven of her eternal spring? to bear the wintry
    rage
Of a harsh terror, driv'n to madness, bound to hold a rod   25
Over her shrinking shoulders all the day, & all the night
To turn the wheel of false desire, and longings that wake her
    womb
To the abhorred birth of cherubs in the human form,
That live a pestilence & die a meteor & are no more;
Till the child dwell with one he hates, and do the deed he
    loaths,   30
And the impure scourge force his seed into its unripe birth
E'er yet his eyelids can behold the arrows of the day.

'Does the whale worship at thy footsteps as the hungry dog?
Or does he scent the mountain prey, because his nostrils wide
Draw in the ocean? does his eye discern the flying cloud   35
As the raven's eye? or does he measure the expanse like the
    vulture?
Does the still spider view the cliffs where eagles hide their
    young?
Or does the fly rejoice because the harvest is brought in?
Does not the eagle scorn the earth & despise the treasures
    beneath?
But the mole knoweth what is there, & the worm shall tell it
    thee.   40
Does not the worm erect a pillar in the mouldering church
    yard,

PLATE 6
And a palace of eternity in the jaws of the hungry grave?
Over his porch these words are written: "Take thy bliss, O
    Man!
And sweet shall be thy taste & sweet thy infant joys renew!"

from **America**

PLATE 6

'The morning comes, the night decays, the watchmen leave
  their stations;
The grave is burst, the spices shed, the linen wrapped up;
The bones of death, the cov'ring clay, the sinews shrunk &
  dry'd
Reviving shake, inspiring move, breathing! awakening!
Spring like redeemed captives when their bonds & bars are
  burst.   5
Let the slave grinding at the mill run out into the field,
Let him look up into the heavens & laugh in the bright air;
Let the inchained soul, shut up in darkness and in sighing,
Whose face has never seen a smile in thirty weary years,
Rise and look out; his chains are loose, his dungeon doors are
  open.   10
And let his wife and children return from the opressor's
  scourge;
They look behind at every step & believe it is a dream,
Singing: "The Sun has left his blackness, & has found a
  fresher morning,
And the fair Moon rejoices in the clear & cloudless night;
For Empire is no more, and now the Lion & Wolf shall
  cease." '   15

PLATE 7

In thunders ends the voice. Then Albion's Angel wrathful
  burnt
Beside the Stone of Night, and like the Eternal Lion's howl
In famine & war reply'd: 'Art thou not Orc, who serpent-
  form'd
Stands at the gate of Enitharmon to devour her children?
Blasphemous Demon, Antichrist, hater of Dignities,   5
Lover of wild rebellion, and transgressor of God's Law,
Why dost thou come to Angel's eyes in this terrific form?'

PLATE 8

The terror answer'd: 'I am Orc, wreath'd round the accursed
    tree.
The times are ended; shadows pass, the morning 'gins to
    break;
The fiery joy that Urizen perverted to ten commands,
What night he led the starry hosts thro' the wide wilderness,
That stony law I stamp to dust, and scatter religion abroad   5
To the four winds as a torn book, & none shall gather the
    leaves;
But they shall rot on desart sands, & consume in bottomless
    deeps,
To make the desarts blossom & the deeps shrink to their
    fountains,
And to renew the fiery joy, and burst the stony roof;
That pale religious letchery, seeking Virginity,   10
May find it in a harlot, and in coarse-clad honesty
The undefil'd, tho' ravish'd in her cradle night and morn;
For every thing that lives is holy, life delights in life;
Because the soul of sweet delight can never be defil'd.
Fires inwrap the earthly globe, yet man is not consum'd;   15
Amidst the lustful fires he walks; his feet become like brass,
His knees and thighs like silver, & his breasts and head like
    gold.'

from **Europe**

A PROPHECY

PLATE 3

'Five windows light the cavern'd Man: thro' one he breathes
    the air;
Thro' one hears music of the spheres; thro' one the eternal
    vine
Flourishes, that he may receive the grapes; thro' one can look
And see small portions of the eternal world that ever groweth;
Thro' one himself pass out what time he please, but he will
    not;   5
For stolen joys are sweet, & bread eaten in secret pleasant.'

So sang a Fairy mocking as he sat on a streak'd Tulip,
Thinking none saw him; when he ceas'd I started from the
    trees,
And caught him in my hat as boys knock down a butterfly.
'How know you this,' said I, 'small Sir? where did you learn
    this song?'   10
Seeing himself in my possession, thus he answer'd me:
'My Master, I am yours; command me, for I must obey.'

'Then tell me what is the material world, and is it dead?'
He laughing answer'd: 'I will write a book on leaves of
    flowers,
If you will feed me on love-thoughts, & give me now and then   15
A cup of sparkling poetic fancies. So, when I am tipsie,
I'll sing to you to this soft lute, and shew you all alive
The world, where every particle of dust breathes forth its joy.'

from **The Book of Urizen**

PLATE 4

   4. 'From the depths of dark solitude; from
The eternal abode in my holiness,
Hidden, set apart in my stern counsels
Reserv'd for the days of futurity,
I have sought for a joy without pain,   10
For a solid without fluctuation.
Why will you die, O Eternals?
Why live in unquenchable burnings? . . .

                                              *

   6. 'Here alone I, in books form'd of metals,
Have written the secrets of wisdom,   25
The secrets of dark contemplation,
By fightings and conflicts dire
With terrible monsters Sin-bred,
Which the bosoms of all inhabit,
Seven deadly Sins of the soul.   30

   7. 'Lo! I unfold my darkness, and on
This rock place with strong hand the Book
Of eternal brass, written in my solitude:

   8. 'Laws of peace, of love, of unity,
Of pity, compassion, forgiveness.   35
Let each chuse one habitation,
His ancient infinite mansion,
One command, one joy, one desire,
One curse, one weight, one measure,
One King, one God, one Law.'   40

                                              *

   4. He, in darkness clos'd, view'd all his race,
And his soul sicken'd! he curs'd
Both sons and daughters; for he saw

That no flesh nor spirit could keep   25
His iron laws one moment.

5. For he saw that life liv'd upon death.

PLATE 25
The Ox in the slaughter house moans,
The Dog at the wintry door.
And he wept & he called it Pity,
And his tears flowed down on the winds.

6. Cold he wander'd on high, over their cities,   5
In weeping & pain & woe;
And where-ever he wander'd in sorrows
Upon the aged heavens,
A cold shadow follow'd behind him
Like a spider's web, moist, cold & dim,   10
Drawing out from his sorrowing soul,
The dungeon-like heaven dividing,
Where ever the footsteps of Urizen
Walk'd over the cities in sorrow;

7. Till a Web, dark & cold, throughout all   15
The tormented element stretch'd
From the sorrows of Urizen's soul.
(And the Web is a Female in embrio.)
None could break the Web, no wings of fire,

8. So twisted the cords & so knotted   20
The meshes, twisted like to the human brain.

9. And all call'd it The Net of Religion.

from **Letters**

From a letter to Dr Trusler

dated 23 August 1799

Fun I love, but too much Fun is of all things the most loathsom. Mirth is better than Fun, & Happiness is better than Mirth. I feel that a Man may be happy in This World. And I know that This World Is a World of Imagination & Vision. I see Every thing I paint In This World, but Every body does not see alike. To the Eyes of a Miser a Guinea is more beautiful than the Sun, & a bag worn with the use of Money has more beautiful proportions than a Vine filled with Grapes. The tree which moves some to tears of joy is in the Eyes of others only a Green thing that stands in the way. Some See Nature all Ridicule & Deformity, & by these I shall not regulate my proportions; & Some Scarce See Nature at all. But to the Eyes of the Man of Imagination Nature is Imagination itself. As a man is, So he Sees. As the Eye is formed, such are its Powers. You certainly Mistake when you say that the Visions of Fancy are not to be found in This World. To Me This World is all One continued Vision of Fancy or Imagination, & I feel Flatter'd when I am told so. What is it sets Homer, Virgil & Milton in so high a rank of Art? Why is the Bible more Entertaining & Instructive than any other book? Is it not because they are addressed to the Imagination, which is Spiritual Sensation, & but mediately to the Understanding or Reason?

'To my Friend Butts I write'

To my Friend Butts I write
My first Vision of Light:
On the yellow sands sitting,
The Sun was Emitting

His Glorious beams   5
From Heaven's high Streams.
Over Sea, over Land
My eyes did Expand
Into regions of air
Away from all Care,   10
Into regions of fire
Remote from Desire.
The Light of the Morning
Heaven's Mountains adorning,
In particles bright   15
The jewels of Light
Distinct shone & clear.
Amaz'd & in fear
I each particle gazed,
Astonish'd, Amazed;   20
For each was a Man
Human-form'd. Swift I ran,
For they beckon'd to me,
Remote by the Sea,
Saying: 'Each grain of Sand,   25
Every stone on the Land,
Each rock & each hill,
Each fountain & rill,
Each herb & each tree,
Mountain, hill, earth & sea,   30
Cloud, Meteor & Star,
Are Men Seen Afar.'
I stood in the Streams
Of Heaven's bright beams
And Saw Felpham sweet   35
Beneath my bright feet
In soft Female charms;
And in her fair arms
My Shadow I knew,
And my wife's shadow too,   40
And My Sister & Friend.
We like Infants descend
In our Shadows on Earth,
Like a weak mortal birth.

My Eyes more & more   45
Like a Sea without Shore
Continue expanding,
The Heavens commanding,
Till the Jewels of Light,
Heavenly Men beaming bright,   50
Appear'd as One Man,
Who Complacent began
My limbs to infold
In his beams of bright gold;
Like dross purg'd away   55
All my mire & my clay.
Soft consum'd in delight
In his bosom Sun bright
I remain'd. Soft he smil'd,
And I heard his voice Mild,   60
Saying: 'This is My Fold,
O thou Ram horn'd with gold,
Who awakest from Sleep
On the Sides of the Deep.
On the Mountains around   65
The roarings resound
Of the lion & wolf,
The loud sea & deep gulf.
These are guards of My Fold,
O thou Ram horn'd with gold.'   70
And the voice faded mild.
I remain'd as a Child;
All I ever had known
Before me bright Shone.
I saw you & your wife   75
By the fountains of life.
Such the Vision to me
Appear'd on the Sea.

from **Blake's Notebook**

(c. 1802–4)

'Mock on, Mock on'

Mock on, Mock on, Voltaire, Rousseau!
Mock on, Mock on – 'tis all in vain!
You throw the sand against the wind,
And the wind blows it back again.

And every sand becomes a Gem   5
Reflected in the beams divine;
Blown back they blind the mocking Eye,
But still in Israel's paths they shine.

The Atoms of Democritus
And Newton's Particles of Light   10
Are sands upon the Red sea shore,
Where Israel's tents do shine so bright.

from **The Pickering MS**

The Mental Traveller

I travel'd thro' a Land of Men,
A Land of Men & Women too,
And heard & saw such dreadful things
As cold Earth wanderers never knew.

For there the Babe is born in joy   5
That was begotten in dire woe,
Just as we Reap in joy the fruit
Which we in bitter tears did sow.

And if the Babe is born a Boy
He's given to a Woman Old,→ 10
Who nails him down upon a rock,
Catches his shrieks in cups of gold.

She binds iron thorns around his head,
She pierces both his hands & feet,
She cuts his heart out at his side   15
To make it feel both cold & heat.

Her fingers number every Nerve,
Just as a Miser counts his gold;
She lives upon his shrieks & cries,
And she grows young as he grows old,   20

Till he becomes a bleeding youth
And she becomes a Virgin bright;
Then he rends up his Manacles
And binds her down for his delight.

He plants himself in all her Nerves,   25
Just as a Husbandman his mould;

And she becomes his dwelling place
And Garden, fruitful seventy fold.

An Aged Shadow soon he fades,
Wand'ring round an Earthly Cot,   30
Full filled all with gems & gold
Which he by industry had got.

And these are the gems of the Human Soul:
The rubies & pearls of a lovesick eye,
The countless gold of the akeing heart,   35
The martyr's groan & the lover's sigh.

They are his meat, they are his drink;
He feeds the Beggar & the Poor
And the wayfaring Traveller;
For ever open is his door.   40

His grief is their eternal joy;
They make the roofs & walls to ring;
Till from the fire on the hearth
A little Female Babe does spring.

And she is all of solid fire
And gems & gold, that none his hand   45
Dares stretch to touch her Baby form,
Or wrap her in his swaddling-band.

But She comes to the man she loves,
If young or old, or rich or poor;   50
They soon drive out the aged Host,
A Beggar at another's door.

He wanders weeping far away
Untill some other take him in;
Oft blind & age-bent, sore distrest,   55
Untill he can a Maiden win.

And to allay his freezing Age
The Poor Man takes her in his arms;

The Cottage fades before his sight,
The Garden & its lovely Charms;   60

The Guests are scatter'd thro' the land,
For the Eye altering alters all;
The Senses roll themselves in fear,
And the flat Earth becomes a Ball;

The Stars, Sun, Moon, all shrink away   65
A desert vast without a bound,
And nothing left to eat or drink,
And a dark desert all around.

The honey of her Infant lips,
The bread & wine of her sweet smile,   70
The wild game of her roving eye,
Does him to Infancy beguile.

For as he eats & drinks he grows
Younger & younger every day;
And on the desart wild they both   75
Wander in terror & dismay.

Like the wild Stag she flees away,
Her fear plants many a thicket wild;
While he pursues her night & day,
By various arts of Love beguil'd,   80

By various arts of Love & Hate;
Till the wide desart planted o'er
With Labyrinths of wayward Love,
Where roams the Lion, Wolf & Boar;

Till he becomes a wayward Babe,   85
And she a weeping Woman Old.
Then many a Lover wanders here,
The Sun & Stars are nearer roll'd,

The trees bring forth sweet Extacy
To all who in the desert roam,   90

Till many a City there is Built
And many a pleasant Shepherd's home.

But when they find the frowning Babe,
Terror strikes thro' the region wide;
They cry, 'the Babe! the Babe is Born!'   95
And flee away on every side.

For who dare touch the frowning form
His arm is wither'd to its root;
Lions, Boars, Wolves, all howling flee,
And every Tree does shed its fruit,   100

And none can touch that frowning form,
Except it be a Woman Old;
She nails him down upon the Rock,
And all is done as I have told.

The Land of Dreams

'Awake, awake! my little Boy,
Thou wast thy Mothers only joy.
Why dost thou weep in thy gentle sleep?
Awake! thy Father does thee keep.'

'O what Land is the Land of Dreams?   5
What are its Mountains & what are its Streams?
O Father, I saw my Mother there
Among the Lillies by waters fair.

'Among the Lambs clothed in white
She walkd with her Thomas in sweet delight.   10
I wept for joy, like a dove I mourn;
O when shall I again return?'

'Dear Child, I also by pleasant Streams
Have wanderd all Night in the Land of Dreams;
But tho calm & warm the Waters wide,   15
I could not get to the other side.'

'Father, O Father, what do we here
In this Land of unbelief & fear?
The Land of Dreams is better far
Above the Light of the Morning Star.'   20

The Crystal Cabinet

The Maiden caught me in the Wild,
Where I was dancing merrily;
She put me into her Cabinet,
And Lock'd me up with a golden Key.

This Cabinet is form'd of Gold   5
And Pearl & Crystal shining bright,
And within it opens into a World
And a little lovely Moony Night.

Another England there I saw,
Another London with its Tower,   10
Another Thames & other Hills,
And another pleasant Surrey Bower,

Another Maiden like herself,
Translucent, lovely, shining clear,
Threefold each in the other clos'd –   15
O, what a pleasant trembling fear!

O, what a smile! a threefold Smile
Fill'd me, that like a flame I burn'd.
I bent to Kiss the lovely Maid,
And found a Threefold Kiss return'd.   20

I strove to seize the inmost Form
With ardor fierce & hands of flame,
But burst the Crystal Cabinet
And like a Weeping Babe became,

A weeping Babe upon the wild,   25
And weeping Woman, pale, reclin'd;
And in the outward air again
I fill'd with woes the passing Wind.

Auguries of Innocence

To see a World in a Grain of Sand
And a Heaven in a Wild Flower,
Hold Infinity in the palm of your hand
And Eternity in an hour.

A Robin Red breast in a Cage   5
Puts all Heaven in a Rage.
A dove house fill'd with doves & Pigeons
Shudders Hell thro' all its regions.
A Dog starv'd at his Master's Gate
Predicts the ruin of the State.   10
A Horse misus'd upon the Road
Calls to Heaven for Human blood.
Each outcry of the hunted Hare
A fibre from the Brain does tear.
A Skylark wounded in the wing,   15
A Cherubim does cease to sing.
The Game Cock clip'd & arm'd for fight
Does the Rising Sun affright.
Every Wolf's & Lion's howl
Raises from Hell a Human Soul.   20
The wild deer wand'ring here & there
Keeps the Human Soul from Care.
The Lamb misus'd breeds Public strife,

And yet forgives the Butcher's Knife.
— The Bat that flits at close of Eve   25
Has left the Brain that won't Believe.
The Owl that calls upon the Night
Speaks the Unbeliever's fright.
He who shall hurt the little Wren
Shall never be belov'd by Men.   30
He who the Ox to wrath has mov'd
Shall never be by Woman lov'd.
The wanton Boy that kills the Fly
Shall feel the Spider's enmity.
He who torments the Chafer's sprite   35
Weaves a Bower in endless Night.
The Catterpiller on the Leaf
Repeats to thee thy Mother's grief.
Kill not the Moth nor Butterfly,
For the last Judgment draweth nigh.   40
He who shall train the Horse to war
Shall never pass the Polar Bar.
The Beggar's Dog & Widow's Cat,
Feed them & thou wilt grow fat.
The Gnat that sings his Summer's song   45
Poison gets from Slander's tongue.
The poison of the Snake & Newt
Is the sweat of Envy's Foot.
The poison of the Honey Bee
Is the Artist's Jealousy.   50
The Prince's Robes & Beggar's Rags
Are Toadstools on the Miser's Bags.
A truth that's told with bad intent
Beats all the Lies you can invent.
It is right it should be so;   55
Man was made for Joy & Woe,
And when this we rightly know,
Thro' the World we safely go.
Joy & Woe are woven fine,
A Clothing for the Soul divine;   60
Under every grief & pine
Runs a joy with silken twine.
The Babe is more than swadling Bands;

Throughout all these Human Lands
Tools were made, & Born were hands –   65
Every Farmer Understands.
Every Tear from Every Eye
Becomes a Babe in Eternity;
This is caught by Females bright
And return'd to its own delight.   70
The Bleat, the Bark, Bellow & Roar
Are Waves that Beat on Heaven's Shore.
The Babe that weeps the Rod beneath
Writes 'Revenge' in realms of death.
The Beggar's Rags fluttering in Air   75
Does to Rags the Heavens tear.
The Soldier arm'd with Sword & Gun
Palsied strikes the Summer's Sun.
The poor Man's Farthing is worth more
Than all the Gold on Afric's Shore.   80
One Mite wrung from the Lab'rer's hands
Shall buy & sell the Miser's Lands;
Or if protected from on high
Does that whole Nation sell & buy.
He who mocks the Infant's Faith   85
Shall be mock'd in Age & Death.
He who shall teach the Child to Doubt
The rotting Grave shall ne'er get out.
He who respects the Infant's faith
Triumphs over Hell & Death.   90
The Child's toys & the Old Man's Reasons
Are the Fruits of the Two seasons.
The Questioner who sits so sly
Shall never know how to Reply.
He who replies to words of Doubt   95
Doth put the Light of Knowledge out.
The Strongest Poison ever known
Came from Cæsar's Laurel Crown.
Nought can deform the Human Race
Like to the Armour's iron brace.   100
When Gold & Gems adorn the Plow
To peaceful Arts shall Envy Bow.
A Riddle, or the Cricket's Cry,

Is to Doubt a fit Reply.
The Emmet's Inch & Eagle's Mile   105
Make Lame Philosophy to smile.
He who Doubts from what he sees
Will ne'er Believe, do what you Please.
If the Sun & Moon should doubt,
They'd immediately Go out.   110
To be in a Passion you Good may do,
But no Good if a Passion is in you.
The Whore & Gambler, by the State
Licenc'd, build that Nation's Fate.
The Harlot's cry from Street to Street   115
Shall weave Old England's winding Sheet.
The Winner's Shout, the Loser's Curse,
Dance before dead England's Hearse.
Every Night & every Morn
Some to Misery are Born.   120
Every Morn & every Night
Some are Born to sweet delight.
Some are Born to sweet delight,
Some are Born to Endless Night.
We are led to Believe a Lie   125
When we see not Thro' the Eye,
Which was Born in a Night to perish in a Night,
When the Soul Slept in Beams of Light.
God Appears & God is Light
To those poor Souls who dwell in Night,   130
But does a Human Form Display
To those who Dwell in Realms of Day.

from **The Four Zoas**

NIGHT 2

'What is the price of Experience? do men buy it for a song,
Or wisdom for a dance in the street? No, it is bought with the
price
Of all that a man hath – his house, his wife, his children.
Wisdom is sold in the desolate market where none come to
buy,   400
And in the wither'd field where the farmer plows for bread in
vain.

'It is an easy thing to triumph in the summer's sun
And in the vintage, & to sing on the waggon loaded with corn;
It is an easy thing to talk of patience to the afflicted,
To speak the laws of prudence to the houseless wanderer,   405
To listen to the hungry raven's cry in wintry season,
When the red blood is fill'd with wine & with the marrow of
lambs;
It is an easy thing to laugh at wrathful elements,
To hear the dog howl at the wintry door, the ox in the
slaughter house moan,
To see a god on every wind, & a blessing on every blast,   410
To hear sounds of love in the thunderstorm that destroys our
enemy's house,
To rejoice in the blight that covers his field, & the sickness that
cuts off his children,
While our olive & vine sing & laugh round our door & our
children bring fruit & flowers.

'Then the groan & the dolor are quite forgotten, & the slave
grinding at the mill,
And the captive in chains, & the poor in the prison, & the
soldier in the field   415
When the shatter'd bone hath laid him groaning among the
happier dead.

'It is an easy thing to rejoice in the tents of prosperity;
Thus could I sing & thus rejoice, but it is not so with me!'

*

NIGHT 3
'Then Man ascended mourning into the splendors of his
    palace;
Above him rose a Shadow from his wearied intellect   50
Of living gold, pure, perfect, holy; in white linen pure he
    hover'd,
A sweet, entrancing self delusion, a watry vision of Man,
Soft exulting in existence, all the Man absorbing.

'Man fell upon his face prostrate before the watry shadow,
Saying, "O Lord, whence is this change? Thou knowest I am
    nothing."   55
And Vala trembled & coverd her face, & her locks were spread
    on the pavement.

'I heard, astonishd at the Vision, & my heart trembled within
    me;
I heard the voice of the Slumberous Man, and thus he spoke
Idolatrous to his own Shadow, words of Eternity uttering:
"O, I am nothing when I enter into judgment with thee.   60
If thou withdraw thy breath, I die & vanish into Hades;
If thou dost lay thine hand upon me, behold I am silent;
If thou withhold thine hand, I perish like a fallen leaf.
O, I am nothing, & to nothing must return again;
If thou withdraw thy breath, behold I am oblivion." '   65

*

NIGHT 7
And Urizen read in his book of brass in sounding tones:

'Listen, O Daughters, to my voice, Listen to the Words of
    Wisdom.   110
So shall you govern over all. Let Moral Duty tune your
    tongue,
But be your hearts harder than the nether millstone.

To bring the shadow of Enitharmon beneath our wondrous
     tree
That Los may Evaporate like smoke & be no more,
Draw down Enitharmon to the Spectre of Urthona   115
And let him have dominion over Los the terrible shade.
Compell the poor to live upon a Crust of bread by soft mild
     arts.
Smile when they frown, frown when they smile; & when a
     man looks pale
With labour & abstinence, say he looks healthy & happy;
And when his children sicken, let them die – there are enough   120
Born, even too many, & our Earth will be overrun
Without these arts. If you would make the poor live with
     temper,
With pomp give every crust of bread you give; with gracious
     cunning
Magnify small gifts; reduce a man to want a gift & then give
     with pomp.
Say he smiles if you hear him sigh. If pale, say he is ruddy.   125
Preach temperance: say he is overgorg'd & drowns his wit
In strong drink, tho' you know that bread & water are all
He can afford. Flatter his wife, pity his children, till we can
Reduce all to our will, as spaniels are taught with art.'

                              *

NIGHT 9
Urizen wept in the dark deep, anxious his Scaly form
To reassume the human; & he wept in the dark deep
Saying: 'O that I had never drank the wine nor eat the bread
Of dark mortality, nor cast my view into futurity, nor turn'd   165
My back dark'ning the present, clouding with a cloud,
And building arches high, & cities, turrets & towers and
     domes
Whose smoke destroy'd the pleasant gardens & whose
     running Kennels
Chok'd the bright rivers, burd'ning with my Ships the angry
     deep;
Thro' Chaos seeking for delight, & in spaces remote   170
Seeking the Eternal which is always present to the wise;

Seeking for pleasure which unsought falls round the infant's
    path
And on the fleeces of mild flocks who neither care nor labour.
But I, the labourer of ages, whose unwearied hands
Are thus deform'd with hardness, with the sword & with the
    spear   175
And with the Chisel & the mallet, I, whose labours vast
Order the nations, separating family by family,
Alone enjoy not. I alone, in misery supreme,
Ungratified give all my joy unto this Luvah & Vala.
Then Go, O dark futurity! I will cast thee forth from these   180
Heavens of my brain, nor will I look upon futurity more.
I cast futurity away, & turn my back upon that void
Which I have made; for lo, futurity is in this moment.
Let Orc consume, let Tharmas rage, let dark Urthona give
All strength to Los & Enitharmon, & let Los self-curs'd   185
Rend down this fabric, as a wall ruin'd & family extinct.
Rage, Orc! Rage, Tharmas! Urizen no longer curbs your rage.'

So Urizen spoke. He shook his snows from off his Shoulders &
    arose
As on a Pyramid of mist, his white robes scattering
The fleecy white; renew'd, he shook his aged mantles off   190
Into the fires. Then glorious, bright, Exulting in his joy,
He sounding rose into the heavens in naked majesty,
In radiant Youth.

*

from **Milton**

PREFACE

PLATE 1

And did those feet in ancient time
Walk upon England's mountains green?
And was the holy Lamb of God
On England's pleasant pastures seen?

And did the Countenance Divine   5
Shine forth upon our clouded hills?
And was Jerusalem builded here
Among these dark Satanic Mills?

Bring me my Bow of burning gold;
Bring me my Arrows of desire;   10
Bring me my Spear; O clouds unfold!
Bring me my Chariot of fire!

I will not cease from Mental Fight,
Nor shall my Sword sleep in my hand,
Till we have built Jerusalem   15
In England's green & pleasant Land.

Would to God that all the Lord's people were Prophets.
                                        Numbers XI.29

[handwritten annotations: "foundations of Christianity", "typography", "built among other man-made evils?", "emotive", "emphasizes Blake's personal desire to bring about change", "calling on for Utopia / empowers the reader", "Echoing Green"]

BOOK THE FIRST

PLATE 14

Then Milton rose up from the heavens of Albion ardorous.   10
The whole Assembly wept prophetic, seeing in Milton's face
And in his lineaments divine the shades of Death & Ulro.
He took off the robe of the promise, & ungirded himself from
   the oath of God.

And Milton said: 'I go to Eternal Death! The Nations still
Follow after the detestable Gods of Priam, in pomp   15

Of warlike selfhood, contradicting and blaspheming.
When will the Resurrection come to deliver the sleeping
    body
From corruptibility? O when, Lord Jesus, wilt thou come?
Tarry no longer, for my soul lies at the gates of death.
I will arise and look forth for the morning of the grave;   20
I will go down to the sepulcher to see if morning breaks;
I will go down to self annihilation and eternal death,
Lest the Last Judgment come & find me unannihilate,
And I be seiz'd & giv'n into the hands of my own Selfhood.
The Lamb of God is seen thro' mists & shadows, hov'ring   25
Over the sepulchers in clouds of Jehovah & winds of Elohim,
A disk of blood, distant; & heav'ns & earth roll dark
    between.
What do I here before the Judgment? without my
    Emanation?
With the daughters of memory & not with the daughters of
    inspiration?
I in my Selfhood am that Satan; I am that Evil One!   30
He is my Spectre! In my obedience to loose him from my
    Hells,
To claim the Hells, my Furnaces, I go to Eternal Death.'

*

PLATE 22
                . . . what time I bound my sandals
On to walk forward thro' Eternity, Los descended to me;   5
And Los behind me stood, a terrible flaming Sun, just close
Behind my back. I turned round in terror, and behold!
Los stood in that fierce glowing fire, & he also stoop'd down
And bound my sandals on in Udan-Adan. Trembling I stood
Exceedingly with fear & terror, standing in the Vale   10
Of Lambeth; but he kissed me, and wish'd me health,
And I became One Man with him arising in my strength.
'Twas too late now to recede. Los had enter'd into my soul;
His terrors now posses'd me whole! I arose in fury &
    strength.

'I am that Shadowy Prophet who Six Thousand Years ago   15

Fell from my station in the Eternal bosom. Six Thousand
   Years
Are finish'd. I return! both Time & Space obey my will.
I in Six Thousand Years walk up and down; for not one
   Moment
Of Time is lost, nor one Event of Space unpermanent,
But all remain; every fabric of Six Thousand Years   20
Remains permanent. Tho' on the Earth where Satan
Fell and was cut off all things vanish & are seen no more,
They vanish not from me & mine; we guard them first &
   last.
The generations of men run on in the tide of Time,
But leave their destin'd lineaments permanent for ever &
   ever.'   25

                    *

PLATE 24
Los is by mortals nam'd Time; Enitharmon is nam'd Space.
But they depict him bald & aged who is in eternal youth,
All powerful, and his locks flourish like the brows of
   morning.   70
He is the Spirit of Prophecy, the ever apparent Elias.
Time is the mercy of Eternity; without Time's swiftness,
Which is the swiftest of all things, all were eternal torment.
All the Gods of the Kingdoms of Earth labour in Los's Halls:
Every one is a fallen Son of the Spirit of Prophecy;   75
He is the Fourth Zoa, that stood around the Throne Divine.

                    *

PLATE 25
Thou seest the Constellations in the deep & wondrous
   Night;
They rise in order and continue their immortal courses
Upon the mountains & in vales, with harp & heavenly song,
With flute & clarion, with cups & measures fill'd with
   foaming wine.
Glitt'ring the streams reflect the Vision of beatitude,   70
And the calm Ocean joys beneath & smooths his awful
   waves.

PLATE 26

These are the Sons of Los, & these the Labourers of the
    Vintage.
Thou seest the gorgeous clothed Flies that dance & sport in
    summer
Upon the sunny brooks & meadows; every one the dance
Knows in its intricate mazes of delight artful to weave,
Each one to sound his instruments of music in the dance   5
To touch each other & recede, to cross & change & return.
These are the Children of Los. Thou seest the Trees on
    mountains;
The wind blows heavy, loud they thunder thro' the
    darksom sky,
Uttering prophecies & speaking instructive words to the
    sons
Of men. These are the Sons of Los, these the Visions of
    Eternity;   10
But we see only as it were the hem of their garments
When with our vegetable eyes we view these wondrous
    Visions.

*

PLATE 28

But others of the Sons of Los build Moments & Minutes &
    Hours
And Days & Months & Years & Ages & Periods, wondrous
    buildings;   45
And every Moment has a Couch of gold for soft repose,
(A Moment equals a pulsation of the artery),
And between every two Moments stands a Daughter of
    Beulah
To feed the Sleepers on their Couches with maternal
    care. . . .

Every Time less than a pulsation of the artery
Is equal in its period & value to Six Thousand Years;

PLATE 29

For in this Period the Poet's work is Done, and all the Great
Events of Time start forth & are conceiv'd in such a Period,
Within a Moment, a Pulsation of the Artery.

The Sky is an immortal Tent built by the Sons of Los;
And every Space that a Man views around his dwelling-
    place,   5
Standing on his own roof or in his garden on a mount
Of twenty-five cubits in height, such space is his Universe:
And on its verge the Sun rises & sets, the Clouds bow
To meet the flat Earth & the Sea in such an order'd Space.
The Starry heavens reach no further, but here bend and set   10
On all sides, & the two Poles turn on their valves of gold;
And if he move his dwelling-place, his heavens also move
Where'er he goes, & all his neighbourhood bewail his loss.
Such are the Spaces called Earth, & such its dimension.
As to that false appearance which appears to the reasoner,   15
As of a Globe rolling thro' Voidness, it is a delusion of Ulro.
The Microscope knows not of this, nor the Telescope; they
    alter
The ratio of the Spectator's Organs, but leave Objects
    untouch'd.
For every Space larger than a red globule of Man's blood
Is visionary, and is created by the Hammer of Los;   20
And every Space smaller than a Globule of Man's blood
    opens
Into Eternity, of which this vegetable Earth is but a shadow.
The red Globule is the unwearied Sun by Los created
To measure Time and Space to mortal Men every morning.
Bowlahoola & Allamanda are placed on each side   25
Of that Pulsation & that Globule, terrible their power.

BOOK THE SECOND

PLATE 31
Thou hearest the Nightingale begin the Song of Spring.
The Lark sitting upon his earthy bed, just as the morn
Apears, listens silent; then springing from the waving Cornfield
    loud   30
He leads the Choir of Day! trill, trill, trill, trill,
Mounting upon the wings of light into the great Expanse,
Reecchoing against the lovely blue & shining heavenly
    Shell.
His little throat labours with inspiration; every feather

On throat & breast & wings vibrates with the effluence
    Divine.   35
All Nature listens silent to him, & the awful Sun
Stands still upon the Mountain looking on this little Bird
With eyes of soft humility & wonder, love & awe.
Then loud from their green covert all the Birds begin their
    Song:
The Thrush, the Linnet & the Goldfinch, Robin & the Wren   40
Awake the Sun from his sweet reverie upon the Mountain;
The Nightingale again assays his song, & thro' the day
And thro' the night warbles luxuriant, every Bird of Song
Attending his loud harmony with admiration & love.
This is a Vision of the lamentation of Beulah over Ololon.   45

Thou perceivest the Flowers put forth their precious
    Odours,
And none can tell how from so small a center comes such
    sweets,
Forgetting that within that Center Eternity expands
Its ever during doors that Og & Anak fiercely guard.
First, e'er the morning breaks, joy opens in the flowery
    bosoms,   50
Joy even to tears, which the Sun rising dries; first the Wild
    Thyme
And Meadow-sweet, downy & soft, waving among the
    reeds,
Light springing on the air, lead the sweet Dance: they wake
The Honeysuckle sleeping on the Oak; the flaunting beauty
Revels along upon the wind; the White-thorn, lovely May,   55
Opens her many lovely eyes; listening the Rose still sleeps –
None dare to wake her; soon she bursts her crimson
    curtain'd bed
And comes forth in the majesty of beauty; every Flower,
The Pink, the Jessamine, the Wall-flower, the Carnation,
The Jonquil, the mild Lilly opes her heavens; every Tree   60
And Flower & Herb soon fill the air with an innumerable
    Dance,
Yet all in order sweet & lovely. Men are sick with Love.
Such is a Vision of the lamentation of Beulah over Ololon.

*

PLATE 32

'Distinguish therefore States from Individuals in those
    States.   22
States change, but Individual Identities never change nor
    cease . . .

Judge then of thy Own Self: thy Eternal Lineaments explore,   30
What is Eternal & what Changeable, & what Annihilable?
The Imagination is not a State: it is the Human Existence
    itself.
Affection or Love becomes a State when divided from
    Imagination.
The Memory is a State always, & the Reason is a State
Created to be Annihilated & a new Ratio Created.   35
Whatever can be Created can be Annihilated. Forms
    cannot.
The Oak is cut down by the Ax, the Lamb falls by the Knife;
But their Forms Eternal Exist For-ever. Amen. Hallelujah!'

Thus they converse with the Dead, watching round the
    Couch of Death.
For God himself enters Death's Door always with those that
    enter,   40
And lays down in the Grave with them, in Visions of
    Eternity,
Till they awake & see Jesus, & the Linen Clothes lying
That the Females had Woven for them, & the Gates of their
    Father's House.

*

PLATE 40

But turning toward Ololon in terrible majesty, Milton
Replied: 'Obey thou the Words of the Inspired Man.
All that can be annihilated must be annihilated   30
That the Children of Jerusalem may be saved from slavery.
There is a Negation, & there is a Contrary;
The Negation must be destroy'd to redeem the Contraries.
The Negation is the Spectre, the Reasoning Power in Man.
This is a false Body, an Incrustation over my Immortal   35

Spirit, a Selfhood which must be put off & annihilated
    alway.
To cleanse the Face of my Spirit by Self-examination,

PLATE 41
To bathe in the Waters of Life, to wash off the Not Human,
I come in Self-annihilation & the grandeur of Inspiration;
To cast off Rational Demonstration by Faith in the Saviour,
To cast off the rotten rags of Memory by Inspiration,
To cast off Bacon, Locke & Newton from Albion's covering,   5
To take off his filthy garments, & clothe him with
    Imagination;
To cast aside from Poetry all that is not Inspiration,
That it no longer shall dare to mock with the aspersion of
    Madness
Cast on the Inspired by the tame high finisher of paltry
    Blots
Indefinite, or paltry Rhymes, or paltry Harmonies,   10
Who creeps into State Government like a catterpiller to
    destroy;
To cast off the idiot Questioner who is always questioning
But never capable of answering, who sits with a sly grin
Silent plotting when to question, like a thief in a cave;
Who publishes doubt & calls it knowledge, whose Science is
    Despair,   15
Whose pretence to knowledge is Envy, whose whole
    Science is
To destroy the wisdom of ages to gratify ravenous Envy,
That rages round him like a Wolf day & night without rest.
He smiles with condescension; he talks of Benevolence &
    Virtue;
And those who act with Benevolence & Virtue they murder
    time on time.   20
These are the destroyers of Jerusalem, these are the
    murderers
Of Jesus, who deny the Faith & mock at Eternal Life;
Who pretend to Poetry that they may destroy Imagination
By imitation of Nature's Images drawn from Remembrance.

from **Jerusalem**

PLATE 4
Of the Sleep of Ulro! and of the passage through
Eternal Death! and of the awaking to Eternal Life.

This theme calls me in sleep night after night, & ev'ry morn
Awakes me at sun-rise; then I see the Saviour over me
Spreading his beams of love & dictating the words of this
    mild song: 5

'Awake! awake, O sleeper of the land of shadows, wake!
    expand!
I am in you and you in me, mutual in love divine:
Fibres of love from man to man thro' Albion's pleasant
    land. . . .
I am not a God afar off, I am a brother and friend;
Within your bosoms I reside, and you reside in me.
Lo! we are One, forgiving all Evil, Not seeking recompense.   20
Ye are my members, O ye sleepers of Beulah, land of
    shades!'

But the perturbed Man away turns down the valleys dark:

'Phantom of the over heated brain! shadow of immortality!
Seeking to keep my soul a victim to thy Love! which binds
Man, the enemy of man, into deceitful friendships.   25
Jerusalem is not; her daughters are indefinite.
By demonstration man alone can live, and not by faith.'

*

PLATE 5
Trembling I sit day and night; my friends are astonish'd at
    me,
Yet they forgive my wanderings. I rest not from my great
    task!
To open the Eternal Worlds, to open the immortal Eyes

Of Man inwards into the Worlds of Thought, into Eternity
Ever expanding in the Bosom of God, the Human
   Imagination.   20
O Saviour pour upon me thy Spirit of meekness & love;
Annihilate the Selfhood in me, be thou all my life!

*

PLATE 31
He came down from Highgate thro' Hackney & Holloway
   towards London
Till he came to old Stratford, & thence to Stepney & the Isle   15
Of Leutha's Dogs, thence thro' the narrows of the River's
   side,
And saw every minute particular, the jewels of Albion,
   running down
The kennels of the streets & lanes as if they were abhorr'd.
Every Universal Form was become barren mountains of
   Moral
Virtue, and every Minute Particular harden'd into grains of
   sand,   20
And all the tendernesses of the soul cast forth as filth &
   mire,
Among the winding places of deep contemplation intricate,
To where the Tower of London frown'd dreadful over
   Jerusalem,
A building of Luvah, builded in Jerusalem's eastern gate to
   be
His secluded Court. Thence to Bethlehem, where was
   builded   25
Dens of despair in the house of bread; enquiring in vain
Of stones and rocks he took his way, for human form was
   none;
And thus he spoke, looking on Albion's City with many
   tears:

'What shall I do? what could I do, if I could find these
   Criminals?
I could not dare to take vengeance for all things are so
   constructed   30
And built by the Divine hand that the sinner shall

always escape,
And he who takes vengeance alone is the criminal of
    Providence.
If I should dare to lay my finger on a grain of sand
In way of vengeance, I punish the already punish'd. O
    whom
Should I pity if I pity not the sinner who is gone astray?   35
O Albion, if thou takest vengeance, if thou revengest thy
    wrongs,
Thou art for ever lost! What can I do to hinder the Sons
Of Albion from taking vengeance? or how shall I them
    perswade?'

So spoke Los, travelling thro' darkness & horrid solitude.
And he beheld Jerusalem in Westminster & Marybone   40
Among the ruins of the Temple, and Vala who is her
    Shadow,
Jerusalem's Shadow bent northward over the Island white.

                              *

PLATE 52
        I saw a Monk of Charlemaine
    Arise before my sight;
        I talk'd with the Grey Monk as we stood
    In beams of infernal light.

        Gibbon arose with a lash of steel   5
    And Voltaire with a wracking wheel;
        The Schools, in clouds of learning roll'd,
    Arose with War in iron & gold.

        'Thou lazy Monk,' they sound afar,
    'In vain condemning glorious War!   10
        And in your Cell you shall ever dwell:
    Rise, War, & bind him in his Cell!'

        The blood red ran from the Grey Monk's side;
    His hands & feet were wounded wide,
        His body bent, his arms & knees   15
    Like to the roots of ancient trees.

When Satan first the black bow bent
And the Moral Law from the Gospel rent,
  He forg'd the Law into a Sword
And spill'd the blood of mercy's Lord.   20

Titus! Constantine! Charlemaine!
O Voltaire! Rousseau! Gibbon! Vain
  Your Grecian Mocks and Roman Sword
Against this image of his Lord!

For a Tear is an Intellectual thing,   25
And a Sigh is the Sword of an Angel King,
  And the bitter groan of a Martyr's woe
Is an Arrow from the Almightie's Bow.

*

PLATE 61
'Behold in the Visions of Elohim Jehovah, behold Joseph &
  Mary
And be comforted, O Jerusalem, in the Visions of Jehovah
  Elohim.'

She looked & saw Joseph the Carpenter in Nazareth, & Mary
His espoused Wife. And Mary said, 'If thou put me away
  from thee,
Dost thou not murder me?' Joseph spoke in anger & fury,
  'Should I   5
Marry a Harlot & an Adulteress?' Mary answer'd, 'Art thou
  more pure
Than thy Maker who forgiveth Sins & calls again Her that
  is Lost?
Tho' She hates, he calls her again in love. I love my dear
  Joseph,
But he driveth me away from his presence; yet I hear the
  voice of God
In the voice of my Husband; tho' he is angry for a moment,
  he will not   10
Utterly cast me away. If I were pure, never could I taste the
  sweets
Of the Forgiveness of Sins; if I were holy, I never could

behold the tears
Of love of him who loves me in the midst of his anger in
    furnace of fire.'

'Ah my Mary!' said Joseph, weeping over & embracing her
    closely in
His arms, 'Doth he forgive Jerusalem, & not exact Purity
    from her who is   15
Polluted? I heard his voice in my sleep & his Angel in my
    dream,
Saying, "Doth Jehovah Forgive a Debt only on condition
    that it shall
Be Payed? Doth he Forgive Pollution only on conditions of
    Purity?
That Debt is not Forgiven! That Pollution is not Forgiven!
Such is the Forgiveness of the Gods, the Moral Virtues of the   20
Heathen, whose tender Mercies are Cruelty. But Jehovah's
    Salvation
Is without Money & without Price, in the Continual
    Forgiveness of Sins,
In the Perpetual Mutual Sacrifice in Great Eternity. For
    behold,
There is none that liveth & Sinneth not! And this is the
    Covenant
Of Jehovah: If you Forgive one-another, so shall Jehovah
    Forgive You,   25
That He Himself may Dwell among You. Fear not then to
    take
To thee Mary thy Wife, for she is with Child by the Holy
    Ghost." '

*

PLATE 65
Then left the Sons of Urizen the plow & harrow, the loom,
The hammer & the chisel & the rule & compasses; from
    London fleeing,
They forg'd the sword on Cheviot, the chariot of war & the
    battle-ax,
The trumpet fitted to mortal battle, & the flute of summer in
    Annandale.   15

And all the Arts of Life they chang'd into the Arts of Death
　　in Albion:
The hour-glass contemn'd because its simple workmanship
Was like the workmanship of the plowman, & the water
　　wheel
That raises water into cisterns broken & burn'd with fire
Because its workmanship was like the workmanship of the
　　shepherd.　　　　　　　　　　　　　　　　　　　　　　20
And in their stead, intricate wheels invented, wheel
　　without wheel,
To perplex youth in their outgoings & to bind to labours in
　　Albion
Of day & night the myriads of eternity; that they may grind
And polish brass & iron hour after hour, laborious task,
Kept ignorant of its use; that they might spend the days of
　　wisdom　　　　　　　　　　　　　　　　　　　　　　　25
In sorrowful drudgery to obtain a scanty pittance of bread;
In ignorance to view a small portion & think that All,
And call it Demonstration, blind to all the simple rules of
　　life.

*

PLATE 91
'He who would see the Divinity must see him in his
　　Children:
One first, in friendship & love, then a Divine Family, & in
　　the midst
Jesus will appear; so he who wishes to see a Vision, a perfect
　　Whole,　　　　　　　　　　　　　　　　　　　　　　20
Must see it in its Minute Particulars, Organized, & not as
　　thou,
O Fiend of Righteousness, pretendest; thine is a
　　Disorganized
And snowy cloud, brooder of tempests & destructive War.
You smile with pomp & rigor, you talk of benevolence &
　　virtue;
I act with benevolence & Virtue & get murder'd time after
　　time.　　　　　　　　　　　　　　　　　　　　　　　25
You accumulate Particulars & murder by analyzing, that

you
May take the aggregate; & you call the aggregate Moral
    Law;
And you call that swell'd & bloated Form a Minute
    Particular.
But General Forms have their vitality in Particulars; &
    every
Particular is a Man, a Divine Member of the Divine Jesus.'   30

So Los cried at his Anvil, in the horrible darkness
    weeping. . . .

PLATE 96
Then Jesus appeared standing by Albion as the Good
    Shepherd
By the lost Sheep that he hath found, & Albion knew that it
Was the Lord, the Universal Humanity; & Albion saw his
    Form   5
A Man, & they conversed as Man with Man in Ages of
    Eternity.
And the Divine Appearance was the likeness & similitude of
    Los.

Albion said: 'O Lord, what can I do? my Selfhood cruel
Marches against thee, deceitful, from Sinai & from Edom
Into the Wilderness of Judah, to meet thee in his pride.   10
I behold the Visions of my deadly Sleep of Six Thousand
    Years
Dazling around thy skirts like a Serpent of precious stones &
    gold.
I know it is my Self, O my Divine Creator & Redeemer.'

Jesus replied: 'Fear not, Albion; unless I die thou canst not
    live,
But if I die I shall arise again & thou with me.   15
This is Friendship & Brotherhood; without it Man Is Not.'

So Jesus spoke. The Covering Cherub coming on in
    darkness
Overshadow'd them, & Jesus said: 'Thus do Men in Eternity,

One for another to put off by forgiveness every sin.'

Albion reply'd: 'Cannot Man exist without Mysterious   20
Offering of Self for Another? is this Friendship &
    Brotherhood?
I see thee in the likeness & similitude of Los my Friend.'

Jesus said: 'Wouldst thou love one who never died
For thee, or ever die for one who had not died for thee?
And if God dieth not for Man & giveth not himself   25
Eternally for Man, Man could not exist; for Man is Love,
As God is Love. Every kindness to another is a little Death
In the Divine Image, nor can Man exist but by
    Brotherhood.'

So saying, the Cloud overshadowing divided them asunder.
Albion stood in terror, not for himself but for his Friend   30
Divine, & Self was lost in the contemplation of faith
And wonder at the Divine Mercy & at Los's sublime honour.

'Do I sleep amidst danger to Friends? O my Cities &
    Counties,
Do you sleep? Rouze up, rouze up! Eternal Death is abroad!'

So Albion spoke, & threw himself into the Furnaces of
    affliction.   35
All was a Vision, all a Dream! The Furnaces became
Fountains of Living Waters flowing from the Humanity
    Divine.
And all the Cities of Albion rose from their Slumbers, and
    All
The Sons & Daughters of Albion on soft clouds, Waking
    from Sleep.
Soon all around remote the Heavens burnt with flaming
    fires,   40
And Urizen & Luvah & Tharmas & Urthona arose into
Albion's Bosom. Then Albion stood before Jesus in the
    Clouds
Of Heaven, Fourfold among the Visions of God in Eternity:

PLATE 97
'Awake, Awake, Jerusalem! O lovely Emanation of Albion,
Awake and overspread all Nations as in Ancient Time;
For lo! the Night of Death is past and the Eternal Day
Appears upon our Hills! Awake, Jerusalem, and come
    away!'

from **For the Sexes: The Gates of Paradise**

The Gates of Paradise

Mutual Forgiveness of each Vice,
Such are the Gates of Paradise.
Against the Accuser's chief desire
Who walkd among the Stones of Fire
Jehovah's Finger Wrote the Law;   5
Then Wept, then rose in Zeal & Awe
And the Dead Corpse from Sinai's heat
Buried beneath his Mercy Seat.
O Christians, Christians, tell me Why
You rear it on your Altars high.   10

To the Accuser Who Is the God of This World

Truly, My Satan, thou art but a Dunce,
And dost not know the Garment from the Man.
Every Harlot was a Virgin once,
Nor canst thou ever change Kate into Nan.

Tho' thou art Worship'd by the Names Divine   5
Of Jesus & Jehovah, thou art still
The Son of Morn in weary Night's decline,
The lost Traveller's Dream under the Hill.

Notes

Abbreviations

B = Blake; *MHH* = *Marriage of Heaven and Hell*; *SE* = *Songs of Experience*; *SI* = *Songs of Innocence*

Poetical Sketches: the Advertisement says the poems were written between B's twelfth and his twentieth year; but if 'Kitty' in 'I love the jocund dance' is his wife, the closing date must be later.

Song: 'How sweet I roam'd: cf. 'The Crystal Cabinet'. **10 Phœbus:** or Apollo, god of the sun and of poetry.

Song: 'My silks and fine array': reminiscent of some Elizabethan songs; but this kind of poem is usually by a male lover.

Mad Song: mad songs were a poetic fashion from Elizabethan times; six appeared in Percy's *Reliques* (1765). **17:** cf. 'Infant Sorrow' 4 in *SE*. **21–2:** cf. 'Introduction' 16–17 in *SE*.

There Is No Natural Religion: directed against empirical philosophy, which holds that knowledge is derived solely from physical sensations ordered by reason.

Songs of Innocence: an early version of 'Laughing Song' was written into a copy of *Poetical Sketches* and early versions of 'Holy Thursday', 'Nurse's Song' and 'The Little Boy Lost' appear in *An Island in the Moon*, written *c.* 1784–5.

The Chimney Sweeper: boys, sometimes as young as four, were sold to sweeps for about £5, and made to go up narrow, sometimes lighted, chimneys.

A Cradle Song: cf. 'A Cradle Hymn' by Isaac Watts, in which the mother contrasts her child to Jesus rather than seeing the 'holy image' in him. Cf. 'A Cradle Song' in B's Notebook.

Night: **37–8 his:** Christ's.

On Another's Sorrow: cf. Cowper's 'Hark my soul! It is the Lord', in which the uncertainty of human compassion is contrasted with the certainty of the divine, whereas here the human points to the divine.

Songs of Experience: most of the poems were drafted in B's Notebook, probably in 1791–3.

Introduction: **9   starry pole:** refers, as in 'A Poison Tree' 14 and older poets, to the whole starry sky. Stars usually have negative associations in B – with Urizen and with Newtonian physics.

The Little Girl Lost and *Found:* originally in *SI*, the change reflecting the ambivalence of the poems. The story recalls the myth of Persephone's abduction into the underworld, understood as an emblem of the soul's descent into the world of generation; and/or suggests the rightness of confronting experience. Cf. *Book of Thel.*

The Fly: there is a deleted second stanza in the Notebook:

> The cut worm
> Forgives the plough
> And dies in peace,
> And so do thou.

The Tyger: **8:** cf. Prometheus, who stole fire from heaven; contrast to the effortless creator of Genesis, 1.

The Lilly: **1–2:** 'lustful' and 'envious' were adjectives tried for the rose, and 'coward' for the sheep.

London: **1–2 charter'd:** originally 'dirty', **8 mind-forg'd manacles:** originally 'German-forged links'. **9 How:** originally 'But most', and this stanza was the last.

The Human Abstract: superseded 'A Divine Image' as the contrary to 'The Divine Image' in *SI*.

To Tirzah: a late addition, probably written about 1804. Tirzah was the capital of the northern kingdom of Israel, a rival of Jerusalem; so used as a symbol of the material as against the spiritual.

The Voice of the Ancient Bard: originally in *SI*; transferred to *SE* in most late copies.

From Blake's Notebook: these poems are near drafts for poems in *SE*, and were presumably written at about the same time.

'Never pain to tell': the first stanza was deleted in the Notebook, but has been restored by most editors.

'To Nobodaddy': **7–8**: in an illustration to *Paradise Lost* B shows Eve taking the fruit in her mouth from the jaws of a serpent coiled around her.

The Book of Thel: dated 1789. Plate 6 and the Motto, in slightly different script, may have been written later, 'experienced' questioning of the 'innocent' lily, etc. **1.1 Mne Seraphim:** in Cornelius Agrippa Bne Seraphim are 'the Intelligences of Venus'. **1.4 Adona:** connected with Adonis, youth loved by Venus. **2.1 Har:** in *Tiriel* inhabited by Har and Heva, an Adam and Eve but existing in a state of self-regarding withdrawal. **6.1 northern bar:** Homer in *Odyssey* xii.109–12 describes the cave of the Naiads, whose northern gate was understood by neo-Platonists as the means of descent of souls into generation. **6.9 grave plot:** earthly life, regarded as a state of sleep or death in contrast to the life of eternity. **Thel's Motto:** on a separate leaf, placed at the beginning in early copies and by most editors; at the end in the last two copies made by B. Appropriately ends the poem with questions. Cf. *Visions of the Daughters of Albion* 5:38–9.

The Marriage of Heaven and Hell: begun by 1790; completed by 1793. **3:** in 1790, thirty-three years after Swedenborg dated the beginning of a new dispensation, and after B's own birth, renewal is coming through the 'hellish' energy of the French Revolution. Swedenborg's writings, seen by B as complacent and unoriginal, are being discarded like Jesus's clothes at the Resurrection. Cf. *America* 6:12. **Edom:** associated with Esau. Esau, Adam, mankind may now be recovering their birthright. **6 Jehovah:** usually in B, as here, a god of inspiration and mercy. **6–7:** B's 'Memorable Fancies' are ironical parodies of Swedenborg's 'Memorable Relations', in which Swedenborg claimed familiarity with heavenly spirits. **Devil:** B himself, using acid on copper plates to reveal his visions. **10.7:** the infant is the unacted desire, better killed than nursed. **14 six thousand years:** placing the creation in 4004 BC, the end would not be far off.

Visions of the Daughters of Albion: written at a time when slavery and the rights of women were newly live issues. **5.3 Urizen:** in his fallen state reason separated from imagination; associated with rulers, moralists, churchmen, etc., who try to impose 'one law'; an element in all of us.

America: **6:** spoken by Orc – the revolutionary spirit of the time; associated with Esau, Prometheus, Jesus.

Europe: dated 1794. This introductory poem, found in only two copies, may have been written later. **3.5   one:** the sense of touch, sex.

The Book of Urizen: originally called *The First Book of Urizen*, intended as the first book of the 'Bible of Hell' announced in *MHH* 24; an ironic parody of Biblical and Miltonic creation narratives.

The Song of Los: dated 1795, when kings from the east were uniting against the French Revolutionaries. **6.9–22:** there were bread riots in England, limitation of wages, encouragement of rioters to burn the houses of the disaffected, etc.; also in London much luxury, delicious songs in Vauxhall Gardens near B's house.

Letters: **1:** Dr Trusler, a prospective patron and author of *The Way to be Rich and Respectable*, had complained that B's work was too unworldly. **2:** written in autumn 1800, soon after moving to Sussex. **3:** in a letter written in summer 1803, telling of his coming trial for sedition, at a time when he was bothered by the fussy patronage of Hayley.

from Blake's Notebook: Mock on, Mock on: Voltaire, Rousseau and Newton, with Democritus originator of the atomic theory of matter, are regarded as believing that the world is made up of particles of dead matter, in opposition to the prophet's vision as given in 'To my friend Butts' 15–33.

from the Pickering MS: in this MS, B wrote fair copies of ten poems, probably written 1801–5.

The Four Zoas: begun about 1795; added to and revised until abandoned *c.* 1807. **2.397–418:** spoken by Enion. Her separation from her consort Tharmas has been part of the fall into disunity of the universal man, Albion. **3.41–65:** spoken by Ahania to her consort Urizen. Man, smitten by inner divisions, projects a delusive self-image and worships it as God. **7.110 Daughters:** anyone who entertains Urizenic attitudes is, to that extent, a son or daughter of Urizen. **9.165 Futurity:** B first wrote 'the past', and in 180, 181, 182, 183 'remembrance'. Brooding on past and future both prevent the vision of eternity in the present.

Milton: dated 1804, but not completed until *c.* 1810. **14.30 Satan:** now the Selfhood, the self-righteous, accusing part of the self rather than the energetic rebel of *MHH*. Milton recognizes the errors of his life and work. Cf. *MHH* 5–6. **22.5 Los descended to me:** enabling B to take on the role of the inspired prophet, and to correct the errors of Milton, who also has entered into him (21.3–14). **28.62–3:** eternity may be entered at any moment, which is then equal to the whole of time. Cf. 22.15–25. **29.11 valves:** halves of a folding door, which open to reveal eternity. **29.16 Ulro:** the lowest state of vision, in which we see only a world of dead matter. **31.45 lamentation:** because Ololon is descending from Eden to Ulro; but the tone is joyful because her merciful descent opens 'a wide road to eternity' (35.35). **31.49 Og and Anak:** obstacles to the entry of the Israelites into the promised land. **32.39 they:** the Seven Angels of the Presence, guardians of men in the mortal condition, into which God himself enters.

Jerusalem: dated 1804; completed by 1820. **31.25 Bethlehem:** Bedlam, an asylum for the insane; means 'house of bread'. **52.1–28:** a development from a draft in the Notebook and from 'A Grey Monk' in the Pickering MS. Deism as the cause of war takes over from the condemnation of vengeance as the main theme. **65.14–15:** Cheviot, on the Scottish border, is associated with war; Annandale with the Druids, practisers of cruel rituals. **96.17 Covering Cherub:** cf. the Cherubim in Genesis, 3.24 who prevent entry to Eden.

For the Sexes: The Gates of Paradise: about 1818 B revised his early *For Children: The Gates of Paradise* and added these two poems as Prologue and Epilogue.